Piceno 91

16⁹⁵

Musical Instruments and Their Decoration

Christoph Rueger

Musical Instruments and Their Decoration

HISTORICAL GEMS OF EUROPEAN CULTURE

Seven Hills Books
Cincinnati, Ohio

Translated from the German by Peter Underwood

FIRST PUBLISHED IN 1986 IN THE U.S. by SEVEN HILLS BOOKS
COPYRIGHT © EDITION LEIPZIG
English Translation Edited by Ron Schneeman

Library of Congress Cataloging in Publication Data
Rueger, Christoph.
    [Musikinstrument und Dekor. English]
    Musical instruments and their decoration.

    Translation of: Musikinstrument und Dekor.
    Bibliography: p.
    Includes indexes.
    1. Musical instruments. 2. Decoration and ornament.
I. Title.
ML460.R833   1985   781.91   84-27667
ISBN 0-911403-17-5

Printed and bound in German Democratic Republic

Contents

Foreword

This book brings together a wide selection of richly decorated musical instruments from the world's most important collections. It is intended however, to be more than a mere depiction and description of a set of 'beautiful' objects. The arrangement and interpretation of the material should help to give the reader a multiple viewpoint—an all-round appreciation—of the individual objects as musical instruments, as objets d'art and also as artefacts reflecting cultural history. As many interconnected threads as possible are drawn together. An additional chapter outlines the history and development of European musical instruments. Of necessity the survey is restricted to stringed instruments, a wide field in themselves as well as the most relevant for our purposes.

The subject is a complex one. It comprises the worlds of music, of instruments and of ornamentation: music, as the most complicated but at the same time most directly emotional of the arts: instruments, as the necessary means of transmitting music—products of craftsmanship that must also obey physical laws; ornamentation, as the manifold artistic decoration of the instruments. One of the main aims of the book is to try to maintain this integrity: the three components are generally given equal weight. Occasionally the stress must vary: when dealing with *barytons* or *tartolds* the focus is

on the unconventional nature of the instruments; in discussing a *harpsichord* from Madame de Maintenon's collection or a *cello* owned by the Duke of Parma, the historical aspect is to the fore, in considering the instrument's biography and commissioning; *organs* give rise to reflections on biblical passages concerning the trumpet; allegorical scenes on the inside of the lid of a *clavichord* transport the observer back to the world of classical mythology; unusual depictions of well-known subjects inspire free speculation. Author and publisher hope that the reader will not approach the book from one viewpoint only—as an expert or maker of musical instruments, as an artist or art historian, as a musicologist, collector or musician—but with the open-minded and catholic attitude of a lover of both art and music.

Two particular aspects need comment. The first concerns the typicality of the instruments depicted—because at first glance the reader might get the impression that musical instruments with lavish ornamentation were the norm. In fact the opposite was the case. Neither our selection nor the stocks of museums can be regarded as typical, especially from the sociological point of view—rather they reflect aspects of the luxurious life-styles of the ruling or propertied classes of their day. Mass-produced musical instruments were normally crudely and sparsely decorated, and those of professional musicians bore little or no decoration. Nevertheless, such sumptuously decorated musical instruments as we have selected in keeping with our own aims tend to be the ones which retain their place longest in museums and in the public's favour, owing to their visual attractiveness.

Secondly, running like a twin thread through our selection of decorative motifs was that dualism which was characterised in classical mythology by Apollo and Marsyas, in Christian churches by the opposition of the sacred and the profane, or religious and pagan, by Nietzsche as Apollonian and Dionysian, and today is represented to some extent by the sociological distinction between highbrow and popular music. Similar contrasting pairs of musical instruments were the *kithara* and the *aulos* in classical times, the *lute* and the *bagpipes* in the Middle Ages, and today perhaps the *organ* and the *saxophone*. The aulos, which will crop up quite often, was a double-reed woodwind instrument which must have had a particularly strident sound and which was often used during the Satyr plays—those sensual counterparts and forerunners of high tragedy. Some idea of its sociological level can be gauged from the "Flaying of Marsyas", a story from classical mythology; this excellent musician was flayed alive merely because his performance enraptured the audience more than Apollo's own efforts on the harp.

To assist comparisons, the range of instruments chosen is limited to the realm of 'elevated' European music since the Renaissance (though we have also tried to include numerous exhibits from the world's leading museums). Instruments with abstract decoration and uniform patterns have not been included as they are of little relevance here. The material—of which an almost embarrassingly rich choice is available—has been arranged in chapters according to the subject matter of the decorations and each instrument is described in turn. This allows comparisons when dealing with related themes. Chronological considerations, systematic structuring and the geographical provenance of the instruments all play a subordinate role.

The History of Decoration

Ornamentation is a symbol of luxury. In the period we are considering, certain aspects of art and craftsmanship were also elevated to the status of luxury. Education, leisure and wealth were prerequisites. Music, which by its very nature can only manifest itself via instruments, acts as a stimulus across a broad spectrum of the arts. This is true in poetry, in ballet and opera, and in the contribution that the instruments themselves make to the fine arts.

The embellishment of musical instruments is an extremely old practice. For example, excavations unearthed a clay drum from the late Stone Age on which certain tree shaped symbols had been painted. Bronze lurs, serpent-shaped military horns with decorated bells, exist from the later Bronze Age. In ancient Egypt (8th dynasty) a silver trumpet was found among the burial treasures of Tutankhamen which, like its wooden case, was decorated with geometric patterns. We know the carnyx, horn of the Celts, from drawings of the late Iron Age. It was bent upwards at the end, with its frightful appearance intensifying the spine-chilling sound. An hydraulos (water organ) from Pompeii is decorated all round with architectural motifs (portals and columns). Quite early on, animal horns were decorated with ornamental patterns. At first, simple lines were etched into them but soon ornate reliefs appeared (oliphants).

In the Middle Ages music was characterised by the treble concept: musica mundana ("harmony of spheres"), musica humana (the ordered structure of the human microcosm, the harmony between body and soul, morality) and musica instrumentalis (music proper). Only the third sphere could be physically perceived. Of the instruments necessary for this, including the human voice, only a few were officially recognised and permitted for ritual and courtly music. In accordance with medieval aesthetics, all three "musicae" were based on the Pythagorean teaching of intervals and proportions. Thus the stringed instruments were clearly pre-eminent. The musical intervals were directly and clearly represented on them and they were the descendants of the acknowledged prototypes of ancient times—the biblical harp and the classical lyre. An English manuscript from the 12th century (St. John's College, Cambridge, B. 18) depicts the ecclesiastical division of instruments into "sheep and goats". Church instruments include the *monochord*, the *glockenspiel*, the *organ*, the *harp* and the *cornett*; in the secular realm Satan is beating the drum surrounded by figures playing the *rebec* and the *horn*. The monochord developed into the psaltery which was the forerunner of the harpsichord; it also founded the long tradition of the sound-holes which developed in many different forms and without which the development of the chordophonic instruments would have been unthinkable. The harp, especially the psaltery harp, was suitable for carving, while the organ, in keeping with the classical tradition, carried designs drawn from architecture in accordance with the prevailing styles of the day. Among the wind instruments, the trumpet was well-liked owing to its biblical merits and its heraldic and military functions. It was often the subject of chase-work.

Secular music gave more scope to the imagination. The now despised hurdy-gurdy sprouted a little carved head at one end. The bagpipes became associated with the devil since the superstition of the day envisaged him in the form of a goat. The rebec became the kit (a pocket-violin). The latter gained a little carved head at the same time and was soon disconcerting the philistines of Europe as the instrument of the dancing master.

The big turning point came with the Renaissance and—of particular relevance to our theme—the fall of the Byzantine empire in 1453 under the Turkish onslaught. The Byzantine intelligentsia and artists fled en masse to the Italian city-states, especially to Venice, unexpectedly enriching the cultural atmosphere there. The Renaissance united, sometimes paradoxically, the hitherto hostile "profane" and "sacred" camps. Angels and satyrs began to happily and even lasciviously rub shoulders and occasionally even exchanged instruments. For example, Leda and the swan might find themselves surrounded by a frieze of angels. Human figures (also in the naked form) and landscapes were by now compulsory elements. Despite this broadmindedness, however, there remained a certain arrogance towards the musical life of the lower classes, whose favourite instruments were likewise looked down upon. Thus Michael Praetorius makes no mention whatsoever of certain instruments, such as the hurdy-gurdy, which had fallen from its place among the noble orchestra of religious instruments to become the accoutrement of the lower class. On the other hand, the Renaissance, which had been largely preoccupied with church music overcame one of the shortcomings of the Middle Ages with the development of the wind instruments. At the same time the spirit of experimentation was also encouraging the extension and refinement of stringed in-

struments which, in view of their suitability for decoration, are of particular relevance to us.

This state of affairs did not change until the arrival of the Baroque age with its exuberant predilection for asymmetry of detail within an overall symmetrical framework. It was grotesque not only in form but also in spirit. Increasingly the musically important parts of the instrument were overrun by the decoration or else they were seemingly alienated from their real purpose. This is especially noticeable with the legs of the keyboard instruments. The sturdy stand with its architectural forms, fast became a lightweight structure which degenerated during the Rococo period into a frivolous jumble of foliage. Pillars and columns became creepers. Deep carvings on stringed instruments (which impair the tone) are rare and date back to the Baroque period; during the Renaissance care was always taken not to damage the instruments.

This proliferation of mainly floral decoration was accompanied by a new and selective musical taste. Many popular instruments of the Renaissance now eked out a bare existence and soon had to give way to the standardisation of the orchestra and the primacy of the violin and harpsichord. On some of the larger keyboard instruments such as the harpsichord and the organ, huge designs were sometimes made with life-size figures of mythological scenes. The self-confident Dutch burghers outshone each other in the ornateness with which they decorated their organ cases. The absolutist rulers increased their display of pomp, but in view of the new orchestral ideal, this trend receded in respect to musical instrument decoration, with a few notable exceptions. This was before the Rococo age arrived and brought the ultimate refinements with a strong presence of exotic motifs.

The almost overnight changeover from Rococo to Neo-Classical-Directoire-Empire was akin to liberation. The return to the equilibrium between function and decoration had a purifying and calming effect. In reaction to asymmetry, there was a return to proportion, straight lines, circles and ovals, though without dropping back into the massive solidity of the Renaissance. After 1750 the Enlightenment reached a peak in the Napoleonic era and ensured a mushrooming of interest in music. By 1800 it had already begun to force the gradual introduction of quasi-industrial production techniques. Hence the individual decoration of instruments at the hand of the master craftsman gradually ceased; they could no longer be produced profitably or in sufficient quantities.

Some manufacturers tried to mass produce decorative patterns, for example, by fixing an engraving (a view of a town or a fashion picture) onto the inside of the lid of keyboard instruments. Certain stereotypes emerged which today are still a feature of mass-produced instruments: lyre-shaped pedal-holders and legs resembling columns in the case of the grand piano. Those instruments which survived into the 18th century despite falling into disuse during the Renaissance—including some with sympathetic strings—now disappeared completely (e. g. the baryton and the viola d'amore, though the latter occasionally reappeared in operas ranging from von Meyerbeer's "Hugenots" to Puccini's "Madame Butterfly"). These had been the most colourful and shapely of stringed instruments.

The aristocratic Empire style was closely followed by the homely middle-class Biedermeier period. The acceptance of the piano as a standard piece of furniture in genteel households led to the foundation of what later became the leading industrial manufacturers of musical instruments. The last examples of individually decorated instruments appeared around the turn of the century and were restricted to prestige projects or experimental productions, which used the musical instrument more or less as a by-product. There was no longer any objective justification for the decoration of the instruments. In the "stile misto" phase, Europe was soon covered with hybrid styles such as the industrial-gothic and the industrial-romantic. Vestiges of these styles lingered on in the world of mechanical musical instruments. Individually decorated instruments experienced one last revival during the Art Nouveau period but were now as unrepresentative as the concert piano which was lavishly painted by an elderly Chagall.

If one were to cast a glance into the orchestra pit during the interval of an opera, one would see only occasional and extremely modest signs of decoration: scrolls or C- and F-holes among the strings, columns on the harps, lyres and pillar-type legs on the piano—if there is one. Even the modern organ cases largely make do without any artistic embellishment. It is not just a question of an economising and rationalising tendency in the production of instruments, but is also the result of a particular tradition which dates back to those doyens of violin and pianoforte construction—Stradivarius and Cristophori. Both men saw the contribution of art towards the construction of musical instruments in a more abstract sense—in the overall design and form. In the course of time this "higher" conception of decoration left its mark on nearly all the descendants of those prototypes (with the possible exception of the pianino, our modern upright piano). We now find instruments attractive even when they are almost totally devoid of decoration.

The Function and Location of the Decoration

Within the history of music the term "total work of art" usually applies to Wagner's musical dramas. In aesthetics and within the framework of our subject, however, it can also apply to the decorated musical instrument. A powerful synthesis of construction, design and ornamentation was formed with the aid of various arts and handicrafts and the completed object generally reflected the prevailing style and taste of the day.

As long als there have been musical instruments, man has attempted to decorate them. His motives have varied. The pagans of pre-history may have wanted to ward off evil spirits or to invoke the gods. The Egyptians were not the only ones who thought of pictures as bridges into the invisible realm of immortality.

One of the original factors must have been the sheer pleasure of the instrument-maker. Later, with the gradual rise of decorative craftsmanship and the visual arts, a formal division of labour took place between master craftsmen and artists. As society developed, the individual personality began to make its mark with its own claims and qualities; consequently, there was an increase in the individual decoration of instruments. It is no coincidence that the most comprehensive expression of this appeared in the Renaissance, the age which epitomised the (socialised) individual; the singular and egotistical decoration of this era was based on a carefree and secular attitude—the self-representation and spotlighting of the artist and creator.

Since the Renaissance, the decoration of European musical instruments has had at least three functions.

Functions

The first is a social and psychological factor and can be termed "showiness". Instruments such as the spinet, smothered with precious stones (Plates 43 and 44), were not only there to be heard, but also had to impress without being played. They were expressions of status. This role as status symbol was by no means restricted to aristocratic milieus. It spread increasingly to the bourgeoisie, reflecting the growing economic and political independence of that class. In a few cases this desire for pomp jeopardised the functioning and musicality of the instrument, for example when a relief was carved too deeply into the back of a stringed instrument, it adversely affected its resonance. In some extreme cases the material itself was unsuitable for the instrument, such as guitars or violins made of marble or tortoise shell.

Larger, more stationary instruments brought a second, basically aesthetic, aspect into play—considerations of interior design. Organs, as the giants of the instrument world, could form integral parts of the interior design of the whole cathedrals. At the same time, stringed keyboard instruments and domestic organs were an influence on the interior decor of the aristocratic salon and the bourgeois drawing room. In this respect, clavichords, harpsichords and pianos proved extremely suitable and adaptable. They were quickly and successfully modified in accordance with the changing tastes. Representing a compromise between the practical and the exotic, certain combination pieces arose, such as the spinet/secretaire, the harpsichord/dresser, and the spinettino/needlework box.

This aesthetic aspect also includes the influence of decoration on the total visual impact of the individual instrument. For example, in animating or breaking up large surfaces, such as the folding doors of organs or clavicytheria and the interior and outer surface of the lids, soundboards and sides of stringed keyboard instruments; to offset the intimidating size of organ cases; or to disguise necessary but unsightly parts of the instrument (e. g. the legs of the harpsichords).

The third aspect, which we may call stimulative, was intended to influence the player whilst enhancing the experience of the listener. In the immediate vision of the musician, the paintings on the interior surface of the lids of spinets were often so expressive and poignant (e. g. an idyllic landscape or love scene) that they must have had an effect on the performance and emotional disposition of the audience. This allowed the piece to be experienced on two levels. Nor should one forget that the art of improvisation, which today has been largely forgotten, was an everyday feature of the musical life of the Renaissance.

When someone like Leonardo da Vinci accompanied himself during a recital of his own poetry on the lira da braccio, which itself often had some fantastic shape (in Leonardo's case a silver horse's skull!), the performance was usually extemporised. It was no accident that the pioneering and multi-faceted Renaissance brought to the European cultural scene not only a rich variety of musical instruments but also the opera: that synthetic species which brought together under the umbrella of antiquity music, literature, drama, dance and the pictorial arts.

In considering the function of decoration, we should also mention the special case of the mute or imitation musical instrument. The lyre guitar of the Empire (though this was actually playable) came to be thought of in the 19th century as the lady's guitar, under the classical post-Directoire influence, particularly of the Napoleonic era, and was soon joined by a mute counterpart—the theatrical prop—which actors gladly made use of during their speeches to produce pathos (as did Schubert's friend, the singer Michael Vogl). Here the outward appearance was the sole conveyor of information and at a purely optical level elicited the requisite associations of classical splendour.

Location of the Decoration

Among the various musical instruments, the keyboards claim the lion's share of pictorial decoration. Strictly speaking, these instruments belong primarily to the chordophonic (stringed) category, though the organ and its variants also belong to the aerophones (flutes and reed instruments). Keyboards were so suitable for decoration because of their relatively large surfaces and, in the case of the organ, the need to break up these large surfaces pictorially and via the use of statues.

The strings on stringed keyboard instruments could be arranged in various ways in relation to the keyboard. On the original horizontal model (clavichord, harpsichord, pianoforte, square piano and the modern grand piano) the inside surface of the lids offered the best area for paintings. Various alternatives were possible depending on whether the strings were set parallel or at right angles to the keys. This latter, original model endowed the clavichord, spinet/virginal and square piano with large rectangular surfaces, whereas the former arrangement gave such instruments as the harpsichord, pianoforte and the modern grand piano a large curved lid over the soundboard reflecting the arc formed by the ends of the strings. The tallest part of the lid, when open, corresponded to the shortest and highest pitched strings. This section of the painting was usually taken up with a graceful group of trees, the depiction of rocks or ruins, or else a splendid view of the open countryside. The longest and deepest strings (on the left) were opposite the short tapered end of the lid. Here the artist often cleverly used perspectives; it is fascinating to observe the ingenuity with which these "dead corners" were often exploited. In the case of the rectangular model, whose strings were at right angles to the keys, the enhancing effect of the painting on the player was paramount since he sat facing the centre of the picture.

In addition to these two alternatives a third variant had also long existed: the vertical arrangement of the strings. The clavicytherium, with its organ-like case, had hinged panels which could be painted both on the inside and outside surfaces, as could the space on the interior of the case housing the strings. The panels of the giraffe piano did not open out and were normally adorned only with supports and overlaid with cloth because of the vibrations. Also, they were integrated into the interior design of the room by being given all kinds of accessories ranging from vases to clocks, especially during the Empire period. Pyramid pianos were less common and more modestly decorated. Their front panels were usually inlaid with marquetry. Decoration of the lyre piano was restricted to the symbolic, large-scale reproduction of Apollo's old instrument skilfully placed so that it contained the frame within itself. The pianino, that variant of the pianoforte which eventually triumphed and became the modern upright piano, was, like the modern grand piano, rarely decorated. The last reminders of a colourful and shapely bygone era are the lyre-shaped pedal-holders on grand pianos and similar embellishments on the upright piano of today.

Naturally, artists not only made use of the inner and outer surfaces of the lid, but also of the sides of the outer case in which the Italian harps, themselves largely devoid of ornamentation, were stored when not in use. In other situations the sides of the instrument itself were used. Here scroll work, ornate heraldic devices and musical instruments were depicted or figures were carved. As a rule, the nameboard separating the keyboard from the wrest plank was also lavishly decorated and sometimes carried the name or coat-of-arms of the owner or customer. Graceful illustrations were usually inlaid with ivory, tortoise shell or precious stones and occasionally even gold leaf. The mottos, testifying to the ar-

tists's humanistic education and outlook, were almost always in Latin, and were displayed either on the nameboard or on the hinged lid that protected the keyboard when not in use from unwanted tampering. INDOCTA MANUS NOLI ME TANGERE—"Let no inexperienced hand touch me!"—was one such motto.

Piano builders in the broadest sense of the word favoured two places for immortalising themselves: the jack rail of harpsichords and spinets (this only became visible when the lid was lifted and was sometimes also decorated and even studded with precious stones) and the roses—those exquisitely carved sound-holes that date back to the psaltery and which represent the historical link between stringed instruments and the stringed keyboard instruments (strictly speaking, between simple and compound chordophones). In the design of these roses, two different national traditions can be distinguished. The Flemish masters, who included the leading Ruckers family, used metal and engraved their initials on the rose; the Italian roses, on the other hand, were of thin wood or coloured parchment and often several layers thick, thus deeply encroaching into the soundboard.

At one time, the legs of the keyboard instruments also formed part of the decoration. The modern grand piano rests on three or sometimes four legs, but the Renaissance or Baroque equivalent had at least five, since the narrow end of the harpsichord had to rest on two legs close together, while the relatively heavy wrest plank, which contained the jack mechanism, was supported by a fifth leg at the point on the right where the typical arc of the belly begins. The legs lent themselves to carving or gilding. Sometimes the legs were disguised as caryatids or atlantes (surviving into the Empire period) or as human statues. At other times, they had the form of pillars or columns. During the Art Nouveau period the true function of the legs as supports was concealed—as in the Rococo period—behind a luxuriant foliage. Some craftsmen connected all the legs together, initially to give the structure more stability and later gratuitously in order to add another visual dimension. Sometimes a platform was laid in between representing, for example, the surface of the sea from which the Tritons were then seen to rise bearing the instrument.

Thus a three-fold optical composition arose: the base of the instrument with possibly a platform; the legs with their connecting struts; in the middle the case, keyboard, nameboard and front flap; and the front and rear lids with their inner and outer decorations.

Very different possibilities and problems arose in the case of the organ. The problem of finding a functional, but attractive arrangement for the great number of large pipes within an overall symmetrical framework was easier to solve than in the case of the symmetrical pyramid pianos, since the windways to the individual pipes could be channelled in any direction desired. Since the Reformation, large organs have had several "storeys". These different tiers were usually marked by columns and figures—normally angels making music. Sometimes the organ case also had folding doors painted on both sides.

After the keyboards, the stringed instruments offered the greatest scope for pictorial decoration. Four areas in particular were commonly decorated: the end of the neck, unless the peg-box was bent back as in the case of the lute; the fretted finger-board (the neck itself); the various sound-holes in the belly; and the resonator.

One does not find large-scale designs. On the other hand, there is an abundance of lovingly created detail. A carved head often appeared at the end of the neck— this was obligatory for the viola and the (courtly) hurdy-gurdy—and here certain traditions evolved. In accordance with their various pitches, the neck of the hurdy-gurdy, baryton, tenor viol and quinton usually terminated in a male head, while the kit and the viola d'amore normally had a dainty female head at the end. The relatively prosaic, if perfectly formed, violin together with its whole family (including some viols) still often bears the motif of a snail on its scroll as a vestige of this tradition. The soundboard of the resonator could not support carvings, apart from a little marquetry, without the instrument being damaged. Carved work was only possible on the tailpiece and, in moderation, on the harder wood on the reverse instrument.

The sound-holes of the stringed instruments ranged from the rose of the lute, which the Arabs brought with them and whose many "arabesques" indicate their origin, via the open, circular sound-holes of the guitar and mandolin to the C-holes of the fiddle and viol, the flame-holes of the viola d'amore and baryton to the standard F-holes of the modern violin.

The back and belly, especially in the inventive age of the Renaissance, were often painted and inlaid. At the beginning of the 18th century, the famous Hamburg master craftsman Joachim Tielke took over this tradition and developed it to a level that was never surpassed.

The finger-board, especially in its broad form as on the lute and baryton, was sometimes decorated with several rectangular ivory engravings.

The most extravagant and imaginative examples in this field were achieved during the Renaissance. The development of the modern orchestra during the age of Bach and Handel made redundant some of the most colourful and unusual stringed instruments, which had offered many opportunities for pictorial embellishment. Among these were some remarkable instruments such as the hurdy-gurdy, the viola da braccio, the baryton and the kit. We must regard this as the price that had to be paid for the stupendous development of playing technique, orchestral music and breadth of musical activity.

An even sorrier picture is presented today by the wind instruments. Among the woodwinds only the recorders sometimes bear carved patterns. Transverse flutes of ivory or porcelain can be valued only as status pieces. Just how vague the term "brass instrument" is can be seen from the fact that instruments carved from animal horn, such as the oliphant, also come under this category, as the sound is produced by the compression of the player's lips. Here there is a long tradition of carvings or scenes covering the whole length of the instrument. Among the true brass instruments, the trumpet was sometimes adorned with fine chase-work at the hand of silversmiths and armourers. This aristocratic and military instrument was sometimes made of silver and partly gilded. The lugubrious and threatening sound of the trombone often led its makers to depict a dragon's or snake's head at its end. In a few cases a metal tongue was inserted into the bell which vibrated in accordance with the passage of air.

Decorative Themes

The following sections deal with the thematic content of the illustrations under eight headings. The boundaries between the categories are sometimes crossed and certain themes are here considered as an integral whole, though they may later reappear in several different sections. For example, a picture such as "Amphyon with the Tritons" might come under any one of the three categories: "mythological themes", "land- and seascapes", or "fabulous creatures".

Musical Scenes

It is only right and proper that our journey through the world of pictorial decoration of the musical instrument should begin with motifs taken from the world of music itself. There are two reasons for their frequent occurrence. First, we must go back to the origins of music in the broadest sense. From classical times music was regarded as a gift of the gods. One of these gods—and leader of the Muses—Apollo carried a harp as his trademark with which he often regaled Polyhymnia—"she of the many songs". A similar interpretation of the use of instrumental and vocal music for ceremonial purposes was held by the Jews and was subsequently adopted by all Christian churches: music was seen as the gift of God and could only be played by those whom the Cre-

ator had endowed with the corresponding ability. This explains why the most popular decorative motifs on musical instruments were scenes of music-making drawn from antiquity and from the Bible. A second aspect came into play during an actual performance: such pictures were supposed to arouse and focus the listener's attention on the act of musical creation visually as well as aurally, while acting as an additional visual stimulus on the player himself. Here self-identification was an important factor. The virtuoso saw himself as part of an exalted tradition and as a guardian of one of the pinnacles of human civilisation. The symbolism of such pictures was intended to flatter and to bring out the best in him.

Among the artists' favourite themes were the famous musicians and singers of the Bible and classical mythology: King David, Apollo, Amphyon and Orpheus (all of them virtuosos on the harp) as well as anonymous representatives of these two realms such as angels, playing either wind or string instruments, and satyrs, depicted only with wind instruments; and real people drawn from various social strata—shepherds blowing horns in pastoral settings or groups of aristocrats situated in immaculate parks or interiors.

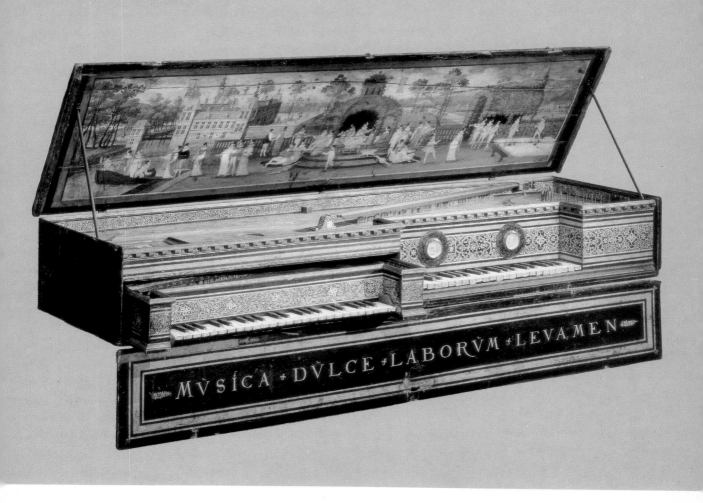

1 Double virginal, Hans Ruckers the Elder, Antwerp, 1581;
New York, Metropolitan Museum of Art.

2 Virginal, Flemish, 1568; London, Victoria and Albert Museum.

3 Harpsichord, Hans Ruckers the Elder, Antwerp, 1573; Munich, Deutsches Museum.

4 Harpsichord, Bohemian, 17th century; Prague, National Museum.

5 Clavicytherium, Italian, early 17th century; New York, Metropolitan Museum of Art.

6 Cello, Domenico Galli, Parma, 1691; Modena, Galleria Estense.

7 Fretted clavichord, German (?), second half of the 17th century; Leipzig, Musikinstrumenten-Museum der Karl-Marx-Universität.

8 Virginal, German, last third of the 18th century; Leipzig, Musikinstrumenten-Museum der Karl-Marx-Universität.

9 Organ of the Marienkirche in Stralsund, Friedrich Stellwagen, 1659.

10 Lyre piano, Johann Christian Schleip, Berlin; Leipzig, Musikinstrumenten-Museum der Karl-Marx-Universität.

11 Double manual harpsichord, Hans Ruckers the Elder, Antwerp, 1612, rebuilt in 1774 by Pascal Taskin; Brussels, Institut Royal du Patrimoine Artistique.

14 Triple manual harpsichord (attributed to Cristofori, 1703), Leopoldo Franciolini, Florence, second half of the 19th century; Nuremberg, Germanisches Nationalmuseum.

15 Harpsichord, Hans (Jean) Ruckers the Younger, Antwerp, 1632;
Neuchâtel, Musée d'Art et d'Histoire.

16 Double virginal, Martin van der Biest, Antwerp, 1580;
Nuremberg, Germanisches Nationalmuseum.

17 Positive, Gottfried Fritzsche (?), German, 17th century;
London, Victoria and Albert Museum.

Previous double page:
18/19 Positive, right and left shutter, probably Nicolaus Menderscheidt,
Nuremberg, *c.* 1635; Leipzig, Musikinstrumenten-Museum
der Karl-Marx-Universität.

20 Spinet, Italian, first half of the 17th century; Leipzig, Musikinstrumenten-Museum
der Karl-Marx-Universität.

21 Double virginal, Ludovico Grovvelus (Grauwels), Flemish, *c.* 1600;
New York, Metropolitan Museum of Art.

Overleaf:
22 Spinet, Domenicus Venetus, Venice, 1566; Nuremberg, Germanisches Nationalmuseum.

23 Organ of the cathedral in Brandenburg/Havel (detail), Johann Joachim Wagner, 1723 or 1725.

24/25 Guitar with detail, Joachim Tielke, Hamburg, late 17th century;
London, Horniman Museum.

26 Viola da gamba, Joachim Tielke, Hamburg, 1691; Munich, Bayerisches Nationalmuseum.

27 Hamburg Cithrinchen, Joachim Tielke, Hamburg, c. 1700;
London, Victoria and Albert Museum.

28/29 Virginal with detail, Gabriel Townsend, English, 1641;
Brussels, Institut Royal du Patrimoine Artistique.

Double page overleaf:
30 Harpsichord, Italian, *c.* 1650; New York, Metropolitan Museum of Art.

Gabriell Townsend fecit 1641

31 Spinet, Italian, *c.* 1600; London, Victoria and Albert Museum.

33 Harpsichord, Dominicus Pisaurensis, Venice, 1553; Paris, Musée Instrumental du Conservatoire.

Group Scenes

Music-making is a collective activity since musical instruments are normally played in a social context. The individual piano dialogue did not become significant until the Age of Sensibility and the 19th century. Although found in all ages as the domain of the creative artist, such monologues/dialogues were always social acts aimed at transcending individuality. Almost all instruments, apart from the keyboards, need to be complemented by other instruments and thus cannot be isolated from a collective setting, beginning with the unlimited possibilities of the musical dialogue.

Most group scenes delight the observer by their strongly relaxed and natural atmosphere, even in courtly settings, despite the strait-jacket of aristocratic etiquette. The reason was obvious: amid all the unnaturalness of a feudal court or an affectatious salon there was a longing for pure, unadulterated Nature.

Allegorical Themes from the Bible and from Antiquity

Among biblical themes, the dramatic stories of the Old Testament featured prominently—Adam and Eve, Abraham, David and Judith. Most popular of all were the series of themes connected with David, the patriarch of church music.

Choirs of angels were often used to denote celestial joy and trumpet-blowing angels were often a symbol of the triumph of the heavenly hosts. On organ cases, the less common themes of the New Testament are also dealt with: Jesus after the resurrection or St. Peter with the key to heaven. On the whole, however, the Old Testament proved far richer dramatically than the stories of the New Testament, which were imbued with Christian charity and stoicism. The central events of the Gospels—the life and death of Jesus—seemed to be taboo to the decorators of musical instruments, except in the case of organs, probably because the basic function of music was to entertain. Portrayers of religious themes generally adhered to the recommendation made by Giovanni Paolo Lomazzo in 1584 that all religious pictures on musical instruments should have a musical theme. The connection between biblical and classical/secular themes was represented by the similarity in the way David/Christ and Orpheus were depicted as well as by the similarity between their lesser equivalents: angels—Muses and their opposites: devils/demons—Pan/Satyr.

Apart from the musical motifs taken from classical mythology, the most popular themes were the nine Muses (usually in association with Apollo) and various gallant scenes from the world of the gods: the complete Cupid thematic, Diana, Leda and the swan, the Triumph of Galatee. Putting it simply, one may say that the main stress was on the power of music and the power of love.

Full-figure Representations of Individuals

These ranged in size from key-length figurines carved at the sides of harpsichord manuals to life-size nude paintings on the inside of lids of grand pianos, and even larger figures on organ cases, which either apparently or actually helped to support the weight above. On vertically strung harpsichords and pianofortes, smaller caryatids often bore the keyboard. In some instances the legs of the harpsichords and pianofortes were replaced by full-sized carved figures or caryatids to heighten the decorative impression.

The most popular subjects were either famous and easily-identifiable individuals like King David or St. Peter or else minor allegorical figures such as angels and demons on organ cases and putti, tritons and sphinxes on the stringed keyboard instruments. By far the most popular anonymous subject of representation, however, was the female form. Owing to the "division of labour" throughout history, this interesting cultural and sociological phenomenon can be partly explained by the fact that the instrument makers, artists and musicians and, in most situations, the customers and owners as well were all men. This male majority determined the subject matter of the decorations. Thus, we frequently find naked or semi-naked figures, both as pictures and sculptures. The stimulational effect on the (usually male) musicians and audience was both considerable and deliberate. The pursuit of art and music was thus also portrayed as a service to beauty.

Organs are also featured in the next section, since their many projections and ledges were used as additional platforms for all kinds of statues, from naturalistic human forms to grimacing demons.

Carved Heads and Portraits

A person's face is an expression of his character. Whereas he can completely rearrange his clothing to suit social conventions or to increase his physical attractiveness, this is not so easy in the case of his physiognomy. He may heighten the effect of his features by means of beard, particular hairstyle, cosmetics and fashion aids but he cannot bring about any fundamental change.

The human countenance is the window into the soul of the personality. Music, as the art which explores the greatest depths, has the most intense influence on the psyche and emotions. It is ideally suited to expressing character via mere sounds, which go beyond the limits of logicality and rationality. Another aspect of this is the personification of the instruments: some of the stringed instruments were even made to resemble the human body.

Carved heads were a feature of most of the instruments that date back to the Renaissance. In the course of time, certain traditions emerged, which we will briefly consider later. It suffices to say that these carved heads, mostly of women, appeared at the ends of pegboxes of kits, viols and, to some extent, on hurdy-gurdies and harps. The viola d'amore was marked by a special feature: it often bore a blindfolded Cupid ("love is blind"). A man's face (often rather morose) was preferred for barytons, the deeper viols and also the unusual treble viol (pardessus de viola), and many hurdy-gurdies. Their features often expressed maturity, intellect and inner nobility—all prerequisites for fully appreciating music, whether as a player or as a listener.

Landscapes, Buildings and Pillars

Goethe wrote in a sonnet:
"Nature and Art at first seem far apart
But really are much closer than one thinks."
Landscapes mirror the soul of the onlooker, capturing his yearning, triggering his memories of past emotions and experiences, typifying his different moods—of sweet reverie, sorrowful parting or surging passion. With their wide range of symbolic expression, landscapes were therefore one of the most popular decorative motifs on musical instruments. The instrument serves to conjure up a world of artistic and aesthetic images and refined sensations, its varied colours, tones and forms reflecting our own moods and enabling us to find enlightenment and comfort. This experience can be greatly heightened by a landscape picture prominently displayed in front of the player or listener.

Among the involuntary images which occur to the listener, those which he has experienced at first hand are probably paramount, either because they are associated with deep memories and hopes of re-living them or because as civilisation develops it alienates us more and more from our primitive roots. These images create an unconscious desire to return to the virgin landscapes of the past, where they are unspoiled by modern technology. Actually this longing is just as old as the deliberate cultivation of antiquity: cultural nostalgia is not a feature restricted to the 20th century.

Many landscapes that one finds depicted on musical instruments are clearly idealised by the inclusion of classical accessories, such as clothing, artefacts or buildings, or by the clear combination of particular landscape elements. Other pictures are estranged from reality by the inclusion of mythical beings or the depiction of allegorical motifs, as we have already seen. In other cases the artist invites the viewer to accompany him on a magical journey into the realm of the exotic: the desire to travel and to see legendary countries was a hallmark of the Renaissance, together with an awareness of the blossoming of the individual personality, a sense of self-respect, and the humanism of the Enlightenment. This was to pave the way for the 18th century rationalism. It is understandable that nearly all decorated instruments made some use of landscape. In almost every picture, the landscape formed the background—complementing, highlighting or underlining particular scenes or motifs.

This section should also include buildings as man-made features of the landscape, together with their adaptable and stylistically variable symbol, the pillar. Urban landscapes ranged from authentic views of towns and semi-fictitious village or castle scenes to pure creations of the imagination. The latter category was usually comprised of intricately and lovingly detailed and meticulously executed works, which could not be appreciated at one glance and were designed more as pictorial extravaganzas rather than as emotional stimuli.

On instruments that stood on the ground, decorated pillars served both functional and ornamental purposes. Here the legs of the stringed keyboard instruments offered many different variations, the classical range of columns being supplemented by pillars, caryatids and atlantes. On organ cases columns were useful for functional, decorative and geometrical purposes. For the harp they were a vital necessity, both as part of the frame and as a means of concealing the inner mechanism.

Chinoiseries

This heading covers scenes of exotic parks and gardens in Chinese style which were sometimes found on musical instruments. Traditionally, the cultures of Japan and China were considered as one, so that the term "Chinese" also covers Japanese culture when considering the introduction of exotic forms to Europe. In any case, the generic term "Chinoiseries" is now firmly established.

Medieval Europe first learned about the "Middle Kingdom" from Marco Polo's journey round China between 1272 and 1295. In 1513 the Portuguese landed in China and in 1520 their diplomats entered Peking. The arrival of the Portuguese in Japan in 1543 sealed the first contact between Europe and East Asia. Even before 1700, the first Chinese products were reaching Europe and becoming all the rage. These included porcelain, lacquered furniture, woven and embroidered silks as well as samples of their magnificent landscape paintings in ink and water-colour on both paper and silk. Thus even before the start of the 18th century, it had become common, first in France and then in Germany and England, for interiors to be designed "à la chinoise". The Rococo period represented both the apex and the end of this development: the playful philosophy of Rococo happily identified with the seemingly cheerful, pleasure-seeking world of China, particularly as they had forms and objects in common (though on closer inspection they can be seen to be basically different). Painted and embroidered scenes from everyday Chinese life (which everyone naturally imagined to be very leisurely) decorated the walls, happily mingling with grotesque designs surviving from the Renaissance. Increasingly "Chinese" vases made by European manufacturers also began to appear in aristocratic salons.

Plants, Animals and Fabulous Creatures

Flowers are Nature's own decoration. Together with the autumn leaves, they form the whole range of natural colours with the possible exception of a few species of tropical animals. Nature's silent world has been verbalised by man; "Say it with flowers" is a common European expression. In Japan, the meticulous art of arranging flowers and rocks has been elevated to the status of a university subject.

The artists of antiquity, searching for natural patterns to copy, made use not only of animal forms (the snail-shell, the ram's horn, etc.) and landscape features (such as the river Meander) but also of a special tropical and sub-tropical plant—the acanthus—which we have already mentioned. As an ornamental motif, it made its first appearance around 500 B.C. in Greece and soon became the trademark of the Corinthian column which spread to the Western and Eastern Roman empire of Byzantium. Owing to its broad leaves, it was often used later by Baroque artists to conceal large surface areas (especially organ cases). In a way, it was the botanical expression of the grotesqueness of Baroque art and, for this reason, it was a popular ornamental motif of that period.

Sometimes flowers formed a decorative theme in their own right, but normally they had a peripheral function of decorating margins and covering large surface areas. Occasionally, we come across floral sculptures, or props carved to resemble plants. Floral decoration and patterns create an impression of gentle and delicate beauty and are thus suitable for highlighting the self-same elements of a piece of music during a performance.

In contrast to floral motifs, those taken from the world of fauna—whether real or fictitious—were normally depicted individually. There were few standard features, apart from the common and obvious association between goats or rams and bagpipes, or between forest animals or horses and hunting instruments. Otherwise it depended on the whim or inspiration of the artist.

The borderline between real and fabulous creatures was often fluid. Before, we opted to put such beings as angels and the Muses into the human category. This was possible because the wings of these "demoiselles inspiratrices" were mere appurtenances to otherwise complete and perfect human bodies. However, this would be impossible in the case of the water-nymphs with their fish-tails or the beautiful half-woman/half-animal creatures.

We have already come across a number of instances of grotesques and of creatures which boldly cross the boundaries between all three realms of living organism—plants, animals and human beings. Such idiosyncratic and weird ornamental motifs were a feature of the whole range of musical instruments during the Renaissance. What was the cause of this phenomenon? It was probably a revolt and escape from an over-governed and artificial society, whose rigid system of Catholic rule excluded any possibility of feedback and hence correction. We can see it as a child-like over-compensation for accumulated frustrations and repressed desires coupled with excessive nostalgia for the supposedly unlimited freedom of antiquity.

Musical Scenes

1 This ornately decorated *double virginal* by the doyen of harpsichord makers, Hans Ruckers the Elder of Antwerp, dates back to 1581. This well-loved, though rather rare instrument, was the precursor of the double manual harpsichord. The octave keyboard with a compass of 4 feet, as opposed to the 8 feet of the virginal, was detachable. It could be withdrawn and placed on top of the virginal and coupled with it. In this instance, this "ottavina" is on the left. In all there are three pictorial levels: the lowered front flap with the motto Mvsica dvlce Laborvm Levamen—"music is the sweet medicine against all ills"; the floral pattern on the nameboard; and the painting itself which stretches right across the inside of the lid.

The painting is a typical product of the Renaissance and consists of a landscape, buildings, everyday life and a musical scene. In this case, it is the everyday life of several aristocrats who are grouped indolently around the central pavilion where the sovereign is listening to the lute. The characters are strolling, dancing and playing a kind of croquet. They are dressed in Spanish fashion, which was the haute couture of the day. The picture exudes an air of leisurely relaxation. Only the servants and court musicians have a stiff bearing.

From the hand of the same master comes this single-manual *harpsichord*. It was made eight years earlier and is the oldest remaining harpsichord by Hans Ruckers the Elder. On the jack rail is a corroboration of this, typically couched in the first person singular as if the instrument itself were speaking: Hans Ruckers me fecit Antverpae 1573. Both case and stand are probably Baroque additions. The colour scheme consists of the ivory-coloured pinewood casing, the gold trimmings on the five curved legs, and the blue and gold on the inside walls and the nameboard. This carries a motto similar to the one mentioned above: Mvsica magnorvm Solamen dvlce Laborvm—which is a strong version of the previous motto: "music is sweet solace in times of great adversity".

At the foot of a flight of stairs in what must be a park (since the figures are unusually large, little space is left for indicating the surroundings), six musicians, dressed in classical style, are singing and dancing. Our attention is drawn to the dancer in the middle. The group of men on the left are painted in the sturdy Flemish style. Note the curious contradiction between the chubby-cheeked yokel and his classical armour. He is playing Apollo's instrument—the harp.

The founder of the Ruckers dynasty (born *c.* 1550, died *c.* 1625) had two famous sons—Hans the Younger (baptised in 1578) and Andreas the Elder (christened in 1579)—as well as a well-known grandson, Andreas the

Younger (the son of Andreas the Elder) who was baptised in 1607. They were all members of the famous St. Luke's Guild of artists to which instrument makers, painters and other artists belonged. Ruckers' harpsichords possessed a particularly fine and silvery tone and were much sought after, especially in England. They then spread via the Spanish to South America. Their trademark was a lead rose showing an angel with a harp, together with the maker's monogram.

According to Greek tradition, the surest way to earn the grace of the gods was by playing the harp/kithara/lyre. Orpheus, who was a harpist by profession, was able to subdue even the Prince of Darkness by his musicianship. Less commonly, he was also credited with the ability to tame wild animals in the same way. Often—too often perhaps—his name has been coupled with that of his wife Eurydice, who made a short-lived escape from Hades.

2   This magnificently carved box-shaped *virginal*, though unsigned, dates back to 1568 and is thus the oldest instrument we have discussed so far. Weapons, trophies and musical instruments have been delicately carved on the walnut case. Elaborate ironwork decoration on the blue-coloured lid interior encloses a medallion showing Orpheus and his transfixed animals. Despite its small size, it dominates the picture because of its central position. On either side is fixed an animal's head holding an iron ring in its mouth with which the instrument could be lifted and carried. It has three Latin inscriptions of which the one at the top is the most interesting. It defines the European concept of polyphony: MVSICA DISPARVM DVLCIS CONCORDIA VOCVM—"music is the sweet harmony of different voices".

The following two plates show combinations of keyboards and furniture. The tradition of designing musical instruments as pieces of furniture survived into the 19th century, and this Italian *clavicytherium* is an early 5 example. It was made by an unknown master at the beginning of the 17th century. Two notable features of this vertically strung harpsichord are its cupboard-like structure, reminiscent of the house organs of the Renaissance (the two side panels open out to form a triptych), and the way the manual is made to resemble a secretaire (the front flap corresponds to the writing sur-

face). Bearing in mind the duality mentioned above, the juxtaposition of King David in the centre as the harpist (Apollo's biblical counterpart) with the four full-bodied female figures on either side is quite risqué. It is surely no coincidence that his gaze is directed towards the more sedate instruments, the treble and bass violins, while he seems to be turning his back on both the singer and the bellicose figure (can we see the smoke of battle in the background?) of Artemis/Athena. And it is precisely she, among this strange group, who is blowing the equivalent of the Greek aulos, here depicted as a cornett—an instrument which was used both in battle and in hunting. Also worthy of note is the skill that the artist used in dealing with the crooked diagonal border separating the central picture from the soundboard. He has placed King David in such a way that at first glance it seems he is actually playing on the strings of the clavicytherium itself.

This *harpsichord* from the 17th century is also un-4 signed and is a combination of musical instrument and dressing table. During a recital its rather squat appearance was to some extent offset by the raised top. The latter is covered with wispy musical scenes: in the centre, Apollo is playing the harp beneath a canopy. In tribute to him, no wind instrument is depicted.

St. Cecilia, the legendary inventor of the organ, was masterfully portrayed on canvas by Italian painters such as Raffael and Dolci. She appears on this fretted *clavichord* from the second half of the 17th century in a 7 very down-to-earth and homely form. Three angels —or putti, to be exact—are singing along and a fourth is "generating wind". On the right, the artist has placed a group of clothed angels dancing in a circle. The lid initially belonged to a harpsichord and was later altered to fit this instrument. This explains the diagonal line in the top right hand corner.

Two musical groups appear on this German *virginal* 8 from the last third of the 18th century. The hinged flap shows a park in which two musicians are playing the bass and drums while a third sings and conducts. The larger picture on the inside of the lid is set in the countryside. Two aristocratic trumpeters are standing on either side of the group seated beneath the leafy shade of a tree in the centre. On the right, the boy with the feather in his hat is leaning on the acanthus as if it were a real fence, as is the third aristocratic musician in the centre of the picture. The Neo-Baroque form and design of the case is of more recent origin—possibly late 19th century.

10 This striking *lyre piano*, which was a specialty of Schleip, a firm of piano builders in Berlin, represents one way in which manufacturers in the 19th century attempted to construct upright pianofortes. The outstanding feature of this instrument is the huge lyre form. Smaller versions recur on all kinds of vertical pianofortes (e. g. pyramid and giraffe pianos) in homage to the legend of Apollo.

9 The crowning glory in this section of instruments decorated with musical motifs is an *organ*, which is one of the oldest to be found on the Baltic coast. It stands in the Late Gothic *Marienkirche*, a church in the port of Stralsund. It was completed in 1659 and paid for by the town's wealthiest guild, the garment makers. Friedrich Stellwagen, born in Halle-on-the-Saale and resident of Lübeck, was given the job of constructing an instrument which would do justice to the impressive and bright building on the west side of the 33 metre high nave. Stellwagen placed the 20 metre-high organ case right under the roof, like a crow's nest, to give added effect to its majestic vertical lines. The organ has three manuals, a pedal keyboard and 51 registers, which testifies to the rich tonal range popular at the time. The same lavish taste is evident in the visual impact of the organ case. The leitmotif is clearly the "heavenly hosts". Musical angels occupy all three clearly-delineated sections. At the bottom the chair organ is flanked by two figures playing the violin amid a bizarre thicket of foliage. The great organ above it has two cherubs playing transverse flutes, though in the course of time one of them has lost his instrument. The central section is dominated by a child conductor. Behind him (one can clearly see his angular harp surmounted by a carved female head) is the figure of King David. The organ above him shows two larger figures playing the cello and violin between smaller gliding angels fixed onto the ornate decoration of the adjacent pedal towers. They are playing a kind of cornett, which for some reason merges with the surrounding ornamentation.

However, the real centre of attention is the group of strident and pugnacious angels placed on the four largest pedal towers and on the top central tower. The angel in the middle is clearly meant to be the archangel Gabriel. He stands apart from the others. In his outstretched left hand, he is holding a shield; it forms a bold diagonal line together with the right arm. Imperiously he is holding a long, straight trumpet like a spear and his wings spread behind him. The secondary angels are blowing looped trumpets, their free hand nonchalantly resting on the hip. The third rank is playing trombones (one can tell this from their raised front arm). For purposes of symmetry, Stellwagen made one of the two "teams" left-handed.

In marked contrast to its position in classical art, the trumpet has been highly regarded in the religious domain since Old Testament times. Joshua used it to bring the walls of Jericho crashing down; in the Holy Scriptures the voice of the Lord is compared to it; and St. John the Evangelist employs it as a symbol of the Last Judgment.

Group Scenes

16 Martin van der Biest, who built the *double virginal* depicted in this picture in Antwerp in 1580, joined the St. Luke's Guild of artists there in 1557—i. e. before Ruckers. It is the oldest extant instrument of its kind. Unlike the similar instrument by Ruckers the Elder described above, which was built just one year later, the "ottavina"—the detachable miniature 4-foot virginal —is this time on the right hand side. The elaborately ornamented instrument makes use of all three of the virginal's surfaces for the purpose of decoration. The soundboard is also decorated with floral patterns. On the inside of the lowered front flap of the ottavina is a medieval French motto: ESPOIR CONFOIRTE—"Hope brings comfort". There are also seven medallions on the nameboard showing: the Governor General of the Netherlands from 1578, Alessandro Farnese; William of Orange-Nassau; the Emperor Maximilian and his wife, Mary of Burgundy; the Orange Princess Charlotte of Bourbon; and King Philip II of Spain with his wife, Anne of Austria. All the medallions are copies of the original moulds.

The medallions are not a random collection. They represent a kind of retrospective review of the complex political situation in the Netherlands from the time of the marriage between Mary of Burgundy, heiress of Charles the Bold, and Maximilian, who became Emperor in 1493 and is commonly known as "the Last Knight". He was the son and successor of Frederick III. By means of this marriage, Spain acquired the Dutch Provinces. Under Philip II's reign, the Provinces seceded under the leadership of William of Orange, who was murdered in 1584. Farnese was the Spanish stadholder at the time. Among his predecessors in the post were the Duke of Alba and Don John of Austria.

The second optical level is formed by a pleasure garden, which was a very popular theme at the time. On either side, the background has been masterfully painted in the Dutch style (a landscape on the left, buildings on the right). The third optical plane is formed by the inside of the long raised front flap. A biblical scene is depicted: Saul in a sudden fit of frenzy chases away David who has been playing for him. Both have bright red cloaks, indicating their highly charged emotional states.

What is intimated in the case of the double virginal takes on a more concrete form on this *cello* by Domenico Galli (Parma, 1691). It also depicts historical scenes, inspired by the Catholic revival under James II. His second wife, much to the chagrin of his Anglican subjects, was Mary of Modena, the sister of Francesco II of Parma-Modena, for whom Galli built both this instrument and the equally sumptuous and ornately carved violin shown on Plate 95. The resentment of the English population grew when in 1688 Mary bore the king a son, James Edward. This dashed their hopes that James II would be succeeded after his death by his Protestant daughters. It was widely suspected that Mary was not the mother of James Edward. The latter called himself James III, but he is better known in history as the Old Pretender. His birth caused a political crisis. James II was officially deposed and fled with his family to France where he died in 1701. Despite several attempts, his son failed to regain the crown, even though he was helped by Louis XIV, the Pope, and the Swedish and Spanish kings. The English parliament placed a bounty of Ł 100,000 on his head.

Domenico Galli naturally gave a pro-Catholic slant to his splendid work—after all, his client was the brother of the deposed English king and uncle of the Pretender. The top-most medallion shows the ducal coat-of-arms surmounted by a crown. The other two are allegorical references to the political situation up to 1691. The larger medallion at the bottom portrays Mary of Modena as a bellicose figure in the mould of Pallas Athena. She is accompanied by a lion representing her son who, it was hoped, would prove the scourge of the Protestants. He is also depicted on the smaller medallion as Hercules conquering the many-headed Hydra—a mythical symbol denoting heresy.

Ornamentation and function are here clearly at odds, for the deep reliefs carved into the soundboard reduce its resonance and hence the tonal quality.

One of the most interesting aspects of the history of musical instruments are the forgeries, which are as old as the renowned names of some of the most famous instruments, workshops and schools. The exquisite triple 14 manual *harpsichord* depicts the coat-of-arms (on the front flap) and triumphal procession (on the wing lid) of a member of the Medici family. Grotesques cover the white case, which is supported by five partly gilded legs. The nameboard bears the legend: BARTOLOMEO CRISTOFORI PATAVINVS FECIT FLORENTIAE 1703. The real manufacturer of this harpsichord did indeed come from Florence, but he lived in the 19/20th century. His name was Leopoldo Franciolini, and he carried on a veritable wholesale trade involving clever imitations of instruments until his prosecution in 1910. He was an accomplished craftsman and dealt with wealthy customers who valued the instruments only as status symbols and antiques. He even had the audacity to have a total of six catalogues printed displaying allegedly restored original instruments. Six triple-manual "originals" by him, plus some simpler harpsichords and clavichords (some of which cannot even be played) are scattered around the museums of the world.

In an age when the harpsichord was already supreme, the *clavichord* survived either because of its simpler method of construction and hence more modest price or because of its particular tonal quality, which was much finer than that of the harpsichord or even the pianoforte. It was thus the instrument both of the man of modest means and of the connoisseur. We do not know the name of the man who made this 17th century Flemish model, but we do know who painted the picture—usually the reverse is true. The painter was Dirk Stoop (1610–1686) and the picture is entitled "A Walk in The Wood". The couple accompanied by a dog are having a stroll in their Sunday best—a characteristic genre painting of bourgeois self-assurance. Behind them, providing the picture with animation and realism, is a "diligence"—a hackney carriage or mail coach. This picture offers a refreshing contrast to the allegorical or idyllic landscapes and scenes of courtly music-making. No doubt the instrument was intended to appeal to the type of burgher depicted in the painting.

It should be noted that this is a fretted clavichord. Such models had up to five keys per string, thereby greatly reducing the depth (here barely 30 cms.). This meant that the instrument was portable and could be carried around. The crooked line of the tangents—a typical feature of the fretted clavichords—is clearly visible.

A few months before she was sent to the guillotine on October 16, 1793 Marie Antoinette, Queen of France and wife of Louis XVI, wanted to do something to comfort one of her ladies-in-waiting—Demoiselle de Trémanville—over the death of her fiancé de Montmollin. He had been a lieutenant in the Royal Guard and had died during the defense of the Tuileries on August 10 of the previous year (information supplied by the Museum of History in Neuchâtel). For this reason the queen pre-

sented the distraught woman with this double manual
15 *harpsichord* made by Hans Ruckers the Younger in
1632.

The instrument is dominated by the large painting
which stretches over the whole length of the inside of
the lid. At the centre of the main lid section is a group of
people stepping into a patch of light shed by the setting
sun. In the distance looms a castle, its outline clearly
visible against the dark sky.

While this typically idyllic landscape may possibly be
as old as the instrument itself, the seven richly gilded
and carved Louis Quinze legs (only one leg supports
the long straight side) were added later. The same
applies to the frieze which runs round the side; scenes
from La Fontaine's Fables are depicted in the style of
Watteau. The ornate designs on a gold background
are reminiscent of the chinoiseries which were at
this time just becoming popular.

11 The next Plate also shows a double manual *harpsichord.* It was built twenty years before the above instrument by Hans Ruckers the Elder in 1612. It was given
its present form in 1774 by the famous Parisian master
Pascal Taskin (cp. Plate 79). The second manual is only
a transposing device altering the key by a fourth. The
creator of the masterful and finely detailed paintings
was the Dutchman Adam Frans van der Meulen
(1632–1690), who accompanied Louis XIV during his
campaigns. Numerous paintings of battles and sieges by
him have survived. The large picture on the inside of the
lid shows the "Sun-King" going out for a ride with his
entourage. On the sides of the case are topographically
exact town views. The constantly repeated theme of an

almost identical group of riders indicates that this was
routine work for the painter.

Among the curios from the history of musical instrument making are a few instances in which the functional aspect is of special interest. Sometimes the layman in
particular is struck by constructions that incorporate
two, usually completely different instruments (e. g. in
the realm of the keyboards an organ-virginal or a
geigenwerk). Then there are a large number of instruments which in addition to their musical function served the most varied supplementary purposes: for example, the combinations of stick and flute (a transverse
flute built into a walking stick); the dressing table-cum-
harpsichord; or the sewing box/spinet.

This *virginal* was built in Southern Germany in the 12
first half of the 17th century. The outside of the lid conceals three drawers and is surmounted by a large pin
cushion. The marquetry of coloured wood and ivory on
the side panels and on the inside of the key front indicate Augsburg as the place of origin. The colourful copperplate engraving which adorns the whole of the inside
of the lid is a "collage" consisting of two quite different
panels—"Spring" and "Summer"—taken from a painting of the four seasons by the Dutch painter Nicolas de
Bruyn which have been skilfully fitted together.
"Spring" shows the aristocratic inhabitants of the castle
checking on how the work on their landscaped garden
is progressing, while "Summer" depicts the grain harvest. The counterpart to the castle is the village with its
church tower and farms. The figures in the foreground
are taking a break from their work.

Allegorical Motifs from the Bible and from Antiquity

Biblical Themes

Smaller organs were subdivided into "portatives" (from the Latin 'portare'—to carry), which really were portable and were carried on processions etc., and "positives" (Latin 'ponere'—to put or place), whose size and weight rendered them immobile. It is thought that the 17 *portative* shown in this picture dates from the 17th century (possibly from the second decade) and was built by the Elector of Saxony's organ-builder Gottfried Fritzsche (1578–1638). The grandson of a professor at Leipzig University and the son of a goldsmith, he lived in Meissen until 1612. In 1603 he built an organ for the cathedral there to replace the one built by his teacher, Hans Lange, in 1580. Fritzsche's organ is still in the cathedral today. Later, he moved to the court in Dresden, grew wealthy and managed to escape the ravages of the Thirty Years' War by fleeing to Hamburg. There he married a parson's widow, Frau Rist, mother of the songwriter/poet Johann Rist.

The paintings on the two side panels deal with the creation of the world (First Book of Moses) and relate the story of Abraham. On the left, we see the banishment of Hagar (Ch. 21): "The slave Hagar is cast out together with her son by Abraham", and, on the right, the sacrifice of Isaac (Ch. 22): "Abraham resolves to sacrifice his son to the Lord". When Sarah at last bore Abraham a son, Isaac, she urged him to disown the Egyptian slave Hagar together with Ishmael, the son she had by Abraham, so that Isaac as the first-born would be his heir. In the desert, mother and son were then saved from death by divine intervention. Ishmael subsequently found himself an Egyptian bride and founded a new tribe: the Ishmaelites. In order to test Abraham again, God demanded that he sacrifice his son. At the last moment He halted the sacrifice. Divine omnipotence, which in both stories—Hagar/Ishmael and Isaac—suddenly manifests itself to the perplexed participants, has been represented here by the two angels in the top corners. In each case, they announce that the Lord has decided to "found a new tribe" with the boy.

The pipes have an unusual arrangement, a diagonal line being preferred to the normal symmetrical pattern. The triangle formed by the remaining free space of the organ case is of high artistic quality. It bears a medallion showing a picture of the client and his coat-of-arms: John George I, the Elector of Saxony, who ruled from 1611 to 1656.

King David was a popular subject for artists, not only in his guise of psalmist and musician, but also because of his dramatic rise from shepherd boy to become a respected and even feared ruler. This Flemish *double vir-* 21 *ginal* by Ludovico Grovvelus (Grauwels) was built around 1600. On the inside of the lid, from right to left, are depicted the fight with the Philistine giant Goliath, the victorious return of the Jews and their reception by the women of Jerusalem.

In the distance, amid a bizarre landscape consisting of rivers and coastland, we see the combat taking place. In the centre of the picture, the hero is returning with the head of Goliath. On his shoulder he carries his shepherd's crook with a bundle at the end. He is shaded from the sun by a canopy held by two ladies dressed in the Spanish ruffs which were fashionable at the time. He is followed by Prince Jonathan, soon to become his best friend, happily bounding along, unlike his father King Saul, who is turning round. This is a symbolic gesture: envy is beginning to gnaw at him, for the young women on the left are singing: "Saul has slain a thousand, but David has slain ten thousand."

The Jerusalem of the Old Testament is made to resemble a medieval German town.

Two Latin inscriptions (including a misspelling of the word 'scientia') are visible when the two front flaps are lowered. Right across the front is the motto: SCIENCIA NON HABET INIMICVM NISI IGNORANTEM—"knowledge has no adversary except ignorance", while the ottavina displays the inscription: ARS VSV IVVANDA, which may loosely be translated as "to enjoy art one must practise it".

The biblical theme displayed on the lid has a pagan counterpart tucked away elsewhere: the two roses show Pan, alias Marsyas, playing his pipes, plus the maker's initials: L. G. The manuals are copiously surrounded by ornate floral patterns.

18 A *positive* from Nuremberg also deals with the theme of David's return, but the two paintings on the interior front panels are more artistic. David is portrayed here
19 as a mere boy while Saul, patriarchal and serious, points significantly at the young hero. The skyline is broken by the frightful trophies of the victor: Goliath's head and armour. David ignores the dancers, who are the first to congratulate him; he is looking out of the picture towards the viewer. The second picture shows the female musicians with a variety of instruments: in addition to the harp, triangle and tambourine, the old brass instruments—bass shawm, cornett and beak flute—are

also visible. Faces, clothing, instruments and buildings have all been painted with great care, indicating the hand of a master. The picture was patterned after a copper-plate engraving by Adrian Collaert, who in turn made use of a drawing by Johann Stradanus which appeared in 1600. An unusual feature of this unsigned *spinet* from the first half of the 17th century is its sexagonal shape, when seen from above. The main picture is based on a popular theme from the Apocrypha: To- 20 bias with the angel (Book of Tobias, Ch. 5 & 6; cp. the last Plate in this book). Surrounding the picture are typical grotesques of the Renaissance: strange fabulous creatures and scrolls.

Johann Joachim Wagner (1690—1749) was a prominent Berlin organ-builder. He built the organ of the *Marienkirche*, the famous church in the centre of Berlin, as well as this *organ* for the cathedral in Brandenburg, 23 which has remained almost totally unchanged to this day. We also know the name of the sculptor: he was Johann Georg Glume, also of Berlin. Two large figures seem to bear the weight of the pedal towers and with them the entire organ case: on the right, St. Paul and on the left, St. Peter with his key to the gate of heaven. His powerful frame effortlessly bears the weight of the timbers and pipes. This can be seen from the relaxed position of the fingers of his left hand and also from the right hand which he raises merely in order to show the key. The artist went to great length to depict the famous saint as a human figure doing a job, since St. Peter cushions the load by means of a cloth over his head and shoulders as if he were a furniture remover.

Ivory engravings depicting the Garden of Eden decorate the ribs of this *guitar*. It was made at the end of the 24 17th century by Joachim Tielke of Hamburg. His specialty were lutes and violas and he was as famous as his contemporary Stradivari. He died in 1719. His instruments were characterised by extremely imaginative designs, the use of expensive materials, and delicate craftsmanship. Instruments built in his workshop usually sold for at least 50 guilders (around 75 thalers). By way of comparison, four years after Tielke's death, Johann Sebastian Bach was granted an annual salary of 100 thalers as choirmaster of the St. Thomas Church in Leipzig by the local council.

In the centre of the picture stands the Tree of Knowledge surrounded by animals. Here they are very docile, as in the story of Orpheus, though later on, they were depicted as wild beasts. Satan has the body of a snake and the head of a girl. Eve has two apples, one of which she hides and the other she holds out temptingly. It is nice to see that Adam himself is shown reaching for an apple while staring, as if transfixed, at Eve.

Mythological Motifs

In Greek mythology, three men in particular were strongly endowed with musical powers: Apollo and Amphion, the sons of Zeus, and the semi-mortal Orpheus, son of Calliope (the Muse of poetry) and either a Thracian king or Apollo himself, depending on which source one takes.

Apollo was the most colourful of the Greek gods. He was the son of Leto and twin brother of Artemis and had a variety of functions: protector of crops and herds, the god of youth, patron of both healing and killing, god of the sun and of prophesy, and patron of travellers (together with Hermes), in particular of the maritime colonisers and settlers. However, the title "Apollo Musagetes" refers to another quite different function: he was also Leader of the Muses.

Apollo with the nine Muses on Mount Parnassus forms the theme for the picture of the lid of this *spinet* built by Domenicus Venetus—"the Venetian"—in 1566 for Count Carlo Bentivoglio of Bologna. This is also indicated by the coat-of-arms plus initials and the friendly text on the nameboard which reads: Vnicvi (que) probo patet praeclara Bentivoglio Domvs— "the house of Bentivoglio is open to all decent folk". The artist has skilfully created the impression that the observer is also standing on Mount Parnassus, for on either side, we see below us distant hills. Apollo, the divine singer, seems a dynamic figure with his lyre and Christian halo. He is accompanied by the nine Muses, who were the products of an embrace between Zeus and Mnemosyne, the goddess of memory—who herself descended from a long line of gods. Although their functions to some extent overlapped, at least three of them were directly connected with music: Euterpe (lyric poetry and music), Polyhymnia (singing), and Terpsichore (dancing). The Muses were proud of their virginity and so were normally depicted fully clothed. Not until the Renaissance did artists begin taking liberties with them.

The instrument is of cypress wood and, with its nine corners, two of which conceal boxes with sliding lids, has a most unusual form, though the iron-wrought outer case disguises this. Apart from a finely carved rose and the ornamentation on the nameboard with the aristocratic owner's hospitable invitation, the decoration is wholly concentrated on the painting which stretches right across the spinet. Four charming girls and a frieze consisting of fabulous animals and ornaments on a lacquered red background enclose the picture. The predominant colour is red: the boxwood natural keys and the sides of the case, together with the surrounding frame described above, all help to achieve the warm effect of this attractive picture.

The love of Zeus was said to be irresistible and brought misfortune to numerous mortals. One of the unluckiest victims was Antiope, a young Theban woman who was brought up by a royal guardian. She bore twins by Zeus—Amphion and Zethus—but was then driven out by her outraged father. Her uncle Lycus, King of Thebes, later made her a slave of his wife, Dirce, after her sons had been exposed on a hilltop. However, they survived and one day returned and killed Lycus. They tied Dirce to the horns of a bull and she was dragged to death (the "Farnese Bull" is a famous sculpture based on this theme). Amphion became king and built a wall around the city with help from his brother and his lyre: while the uncouth Zethus hauled up the stones, Amphion magically caused the stones to form themselves into a wall by playing on his lyre.

As a half-god Amphion felt at home surrounded by fabulous creatures. Built around 1600, the lid of this

31 Italian *spinet*, which strictly speaking is a spinettino or ottavina since it is an octave higher than normal pitch, has a painting of Amphion amid amorous tritons and nymphs. He is riding on a goggle-eyed dolphin and is deeply engrossed in playing a large viola. On his head is a wreath of ivy; his white cloak, strangely, is blowing the wrong way (the full sails of the three-master are pointed in the opposite direction). The triangular case, which this time is the same shape as the instrument, is responsible for the unusual trapezoid form of the painting. To the left, three female beauties on a giant mussel claim our attention. In such a context the presence of the carefully detailed frigate, with its passengers who are observing the wondrous events at their leisure is a little odd. Of the other decoration, the fine gilding on a black background on the nameboard is worthy of mention. It contains allegorical figures painted lightly and daintily in the manner of Pompeian frescoes.

The third famous musical figure of Greek mythology was Orpheus, who was very much in the same mould as his father Apollo. He was allotted a most wretched fate. His wife Eurydice died as a result of a snake bite, but because of the beautiful way he played the lyre Persephone relented for once and allowed the loving husband to take his wife out of Hades and back to the living world. However, when he broke his promise not to look back he lost her forever. The widower journied through distant countries and—a worthy son of his father—introduced religion and law as civilising influences everywhere he went. As an old man, he even accompanied the Argonauts to Colchis. Finally, he wandered disconsolately through Thracia thinking only of his Eurydice. This so angered a band of Bacchantes that they tore him to shreds. But the gods fixed his lyre in heaven as a star, thus giving him an eternal memorial.

29 Orpheus normally appears on musical instruments accompanied by wild beasts which, spellbound by the sound of his lyre, suddenly become docile. It was probably thought that the dark depths of hell were an unsuitable theme for a picture intended to inspire musicality, or maybe the artists were stimulated by the variety of exhibits on show in the local zoo.

28 The oldest extant English *virginal* was built by Gabriel Townsend in 1641. A large rectangular lid interior surface again forms the canvas, on which the artist has painted an unusual, naive-type picture. Snapshots of typically English park and coastal scenes adorn the lowered front flap. Of interest is the identity of the first owner: in several places the monogram E. R. appears together with the coat-of-arms of the English crown. They must mean "Elizabeth Regina" but cannot refer to the famous queen since she died in 1603. The experts believe it is a reference to the daughter of James I, Elizabeth Stuart (granddaughter of Mary Stuart), who in 1613, much to the delight of her fellow countrymen, married Frederick V, the elector palatine. Owing to the short duration of his reign, the latter was given the nickname "the Winter-King".

Sometimes forgers committed incredible blunders. This *Hamburg cithrinchen*, a bell-shaped cittern (nor- 27 mally they were pear-shaped) with five double courses of strings and a slightly arched back, bears in two different places the inscription "Joachim Tielke in Hamburg, 1539", although the date has clearly been added by a different hand. In reality, the instrument was built around 1700. From 1669, Tielke was the greatest lutemaker of his time and a resident of Hamburg. We can only presume that the cittern fell into the hands of some philistine who, in order to re-sell it at a profit, simply antedated it by 200 years without even bothering to check the rudimentary biographical details of Tielke who, even at that time, was famous.

The surface of this superb instrument, a member of the fiddle family, is covered with marquetry of tortoise shell and ivory and gems of coloured glass. Floral patterns cover both sides of the soundbox, the ribs and the reverse of the neck and peg-box, which has a wooden finial in the form of a woman's head. The two scenes on the back form the centre of attraction. One shows the triumphal procession of the beautiful nymph Galatea, who is riding on a carriage which is being pulled by dolphins surmounted by amorettes. Facing it is a similar scene set on land: Artemis leans back gracefully in her carriage which is being pulled along at breakneck speed by two deer. Cupid, the little god of love and general mischief-maker, appears again on the reverse of the neck, evidently taking his leave of his mother Venus. The meaning is clear: whether on land or at sea, love is always the aim of the chase, and love is also the last trump.

Like the above mentioned bell-cittern, this *viola da gamba* was also made by Tielke, in 1691. Apart from the belly, which had to remain resonant, it is also completely covered by engravings of ivory, ebony, tortoise shell, silver and mother-of-pearl. Its carved head of ivory, representing Artemis, is dealt with below (see Pl. 58). The back of the instrument shows white figures on a black background—on the neck and ribs it is the other way round. The parallels between the two instruments (cp. the figures of Cupid and Artemis) show that they were made in the same workshop. Six medallions are set against a slightly wobbly chequered background. The picture below the neck depicts a musician (now headless) who is playing a viola da gamba. He is surrounded by a fantastic mixture of flora and fauna: animals are shown growing out of exotic flowers. The next scenes all feature Cupid. One shows him shooting an arrow at a captive victim who has a target fixed to his chest; in the next he is attacking Ares, his mother's lover and his own father, with his bow while Venus herself looks on; and, in the third picture, he is robbing a bearded warrior of his sword. His charm enabled him to overcome even the leaders of the Olympian hierarchy since they were glad to avail themselves of his services in order to inflame their waning passions.

The two large medallions on the lower bouts each show a god riding in a chariot: on the left, the bearded Cronus and on the right, a boyish Artemis. His realm is the night and the crescent moon and hers the daytime and the sun. Later she increased her responsibilities and became goddess of the moon—hence the crescent above her head. The two pictures form a poignant contrast, just like the colour tone mentioned above.

It is interesting to compare this viol with the cittern. The viol has been much more delicately decorated: the figure of Artemis, goddess of hunting, chastity and the moon, has been treated much more finely (both pictures were clearly based on the same model); Cupid has been given a definite function as the driver of the team; the head of the deer which is turning round is better proportioned and more carefully worked. The two largest

medallions each carry a lightly etched motto, though the language is a mishmash of Latin, Italian and English, reflecting Hamburg's cosmopolitan status. Beneath Cronus, the god of time, is the motto: HARDY ET PROMPT. Below Artemis, not surprisingly, is an erotic caption: VINCE OGNI COSA AMORE—"Conquer everything through love".

The Italian instrument maker, Alessandro Trasuntino, is known to have been in Venice in 1531–1538 and 1604. In 1537 he built two fretted *clavichords*, which are the oldest surviving such instruments. The experts believe that the clavichord shown in our picture was altered by a Flemish or German master in the 17th century. However, the inscription on the interior walls, the outer Renaissance frieze, and the delicate ivory marquetry on the nameboard—showing a stylised crown between two meticulously embossed oblong patterns—all seem authentic. Separating the two parts of the inscription is a Latin proverb with some of the letters omitted: VT ROSA FLOS FLORVM ITA HOC CLAVIE CLAVILIVM—"Just as the rose is the flower among flowers, so this is the instrument among the instruments".

The painting on the lid interior depicts the classical theme of Leda and the swan. Despite its somewhat lascivious nature, two angels are also present and are happily playing shawms (the equivalent of the classical aulos). Each is flanked by a dancer and a creature which is half putto and half sea-horse from whose tail flowers are dangling. Leda, granddaughter of Ares and mother of Clytemnestra, is looking rather anxiously at the swan, which is really the god Zeus in disguise. Her wariness is understandable since mortals rarely escaped unscathed from an encounter with Zeus. In Leda's case, it led to the conception of two eggs from one of which emerged the beautiful Helen, who helped to spark the Trojan War!

Two interesting things should be noted with respect to the colour scheme. Firstly, the artist preferred to sharply delineate the colours; this is evident in the segments which form semi-circles in the four corners and by the "butterfly wings" which enclose the central picture. Grotesques are used to good effect on the light panels both on the sides of the instrument and on the lid by each side of the medallion. Secondly, we should notice the contrast of red and blue inside the afore-mentioned light panels—the clothing of the angels, the ribbons of the putti and even the calyces of the flowers all complement one another.

The fact that Italian harpsichords normally had an outer case—the only part of the instrument to be lavishly decorated—sometimes led to this case being exchanged in later years for a more modern or ornate one.

33 One such example is this *harpsichord* built by Dominicus Pisaurensis in Venice in 1553: the outer case is from the 17th century. Dominicus was born in Rossini's town, Pesaro (known as Pisaurum in Roman times) and lived in Venice from 1548. Instruments by him have survived from 1553 and 1575. He was considered a fine instrument-maker even during his own life-time; consequently, a number of forgers tried to imitate his "signature".

An allegorical painting covers the whole length of the inside surface of the lid even including the foremost flap. It shows Comedy (with the mask), Tragedy (with the dagger—a somewhat dramatic but clear symbol), Poetry (an inspired figure adjacent to Music; the two are of course closely related), and Music. Music is watching Poetry with rapt attention; she has a pen in her hand as if Poetry were dictating something to her. Music's instrument and score are prominently displayed. Both Music and Comedy appear to be female.

30 In Italy a *harpsichord* was made in 1650 by an accomplished master of his trade. It really deserves a chapter all to itself since it is a multiple work of art consisting of a musical instrument and a magnificent sculpture. However, it was actually only one third of a mechanised musical ensemble consisting of three parts which was dubbed "Macchina di Polifemo e Galatea" by Michele Todini in 1676.

The centre-piece of the combination, all parts of which are gilt, is the harpsichord borne on the shoulders of three tritons who, being out of their natural element, must find the weight of the instrument a double burden. The voluptuous nereids are two-thirds out of the water, symbolised by a platform with imitation waves resting on a series of Baroque claws. Bringing up

the rear is a putto on a mussel-shell carried by two dolphins. Originally, his hands probably held reins.

On either side of the harpsichord are two life-size sculptures: on the left, Polyphemus with a set of bagpipes (another descendant of the aulos); on the right, Galatea, naked except for a veil. From the position of her hands it seems that she originally held a lute. Legend has it that Galatea, a beautiful nereid or sea-nymph, was unsuccessfully wooed by a wild and clumsy cyclops called Polyphemus. Later, when Homer wrote about him, he was one of the man-eating one-eyed shepherds who originally inhabited Cicily and gave Odysseus and his companions an extremely unfriendly reception. His clumsy attempt to court the delectable Galatea, whose triumph is depicted separately on the frieze on the side of the harpsichord (see below), inspired many classical poets such as Theocritus and Ovid.

Here the cyclops does not look at all fierce, but rather distraught because his pleas have fallen on deaf ears. A set of concealed pipes ran from the harpsichord to the rock beneath Polyphemus, so his bagpipe could be made to produce real music. We should also note the reappearance of the old dualism: Polyphemus, though here to some extent tamed by the pangs of love, is a rough and uncouth figure in the mould of Pan and Marsyas and holds a modern and more powerful version of the aulos. The graceful and refined Galatea, on the other hand, has Apollo's old instrument. And between the two poles sits the mediating figure of the musician.

Finally, a word should be said about the richly detailed carving on the near side of the harpsichord case. It supplements the main theme and depicts the triumphal procession of Galatea seated in a carriage made of shells and pulled by fish-tailed horses along the sea's surface. She is accompanied by trumpet-blowing tritons. On the far left directly above the strained face of the triton-statue is a team of three excited horses. Next to them is a young lute-player sitting, like Polyphemus, on a rock, but in contrast to Polyphemus, he is tranquil and engrossed in the music; the pair represent the dialectical unity of the Dionysian and the Apollonian.

34 Kit, German, 1690; Copenhagen, Musikhistorisk Museum.

35/36 Kit, front and back, Karel B. Dvořak, Prague, late 19th century;
Prague, National Museum.

39 Organ of the cathedral in Freiberg, Saxony (detail), Gottfried Silbermann, 1714.
40 Harpsichord, Venice, 18th century; Copenhagen, Musikhistorisk Museum.

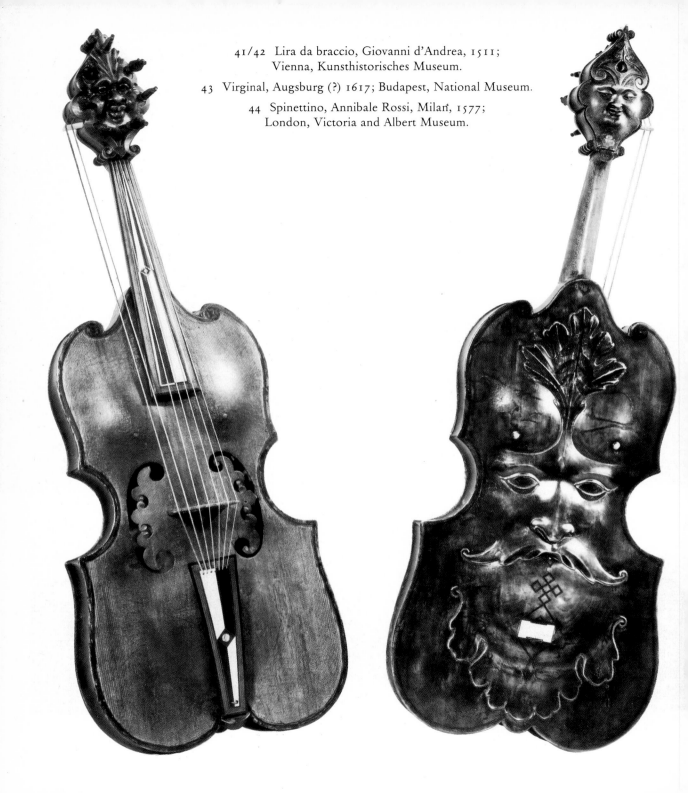

41/42 Lira da braccio, Giovanni d'Andrea, 1511;
Vienna, Kunsthistorisches Museum.

43 Virginal, Augsburg (?) 1617; Budapest, National Museum.

44 Spinettino, Annibale Rossi, Milan, 1577;
London, Victoria and Albert Museum.

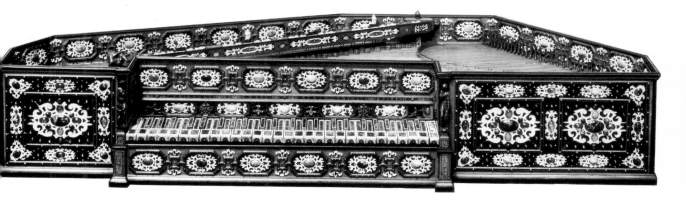

45 Concert grand, Alexandre Charpentier, French, 1902;
   Nice, Musée des Beaux-Arts Jules Chéret.

46 Organ of the Bachkirche in Arnstadt, Thuringia, 1703.

47 Viola d'amore, Tomaš Ondřej Hulinzký, Prague, 1769; Prague, National Museum.

48 Violin, Jean Baptiste Vuillaume, Paris, 19th century; Prague, National Museum.

51 Kit, German, 1690; Copenhagen, Musikhistorisk Museum.

52 Viola d'amore (detail), Kaspar Stadler, Munich, 1714; Nuremberg, Germanisches Nationalmuseum.

53 Viola d'amore (detail), Franz Geissenhof, Vienna, 1779; Leipzig, Musikinstrumenten-Museum der Karl-Marx-Universität.

57 Pedal-harp (detail), Jean Henri Naderman, Paris, 1785; London, Victoria and Albert Museum.

58 Viola da gamba (detail), Joachim Tielke, Hamburg, 1691; Munich, Bayerisches Nationalmuseum.

59 Alto gamba (detail), Johann Christian Hoffmann, Leipzig, 1731; Leipzig, Musikinstrumenten-Museum der Karl-Marx-Universität.

Overleaf:
60 Chordophone, Clauss & Co., Leipzig, c. 1900;
Leipzig, Musikinstrumenten-Museum der Karl-Marx-Universität.

61 Tenor viol (detail), Thomas Edlinger the Elder, Augsburg, 1672;
Leipzig, Musikinstrumenten-Museum der Karl-Marx-Universität.

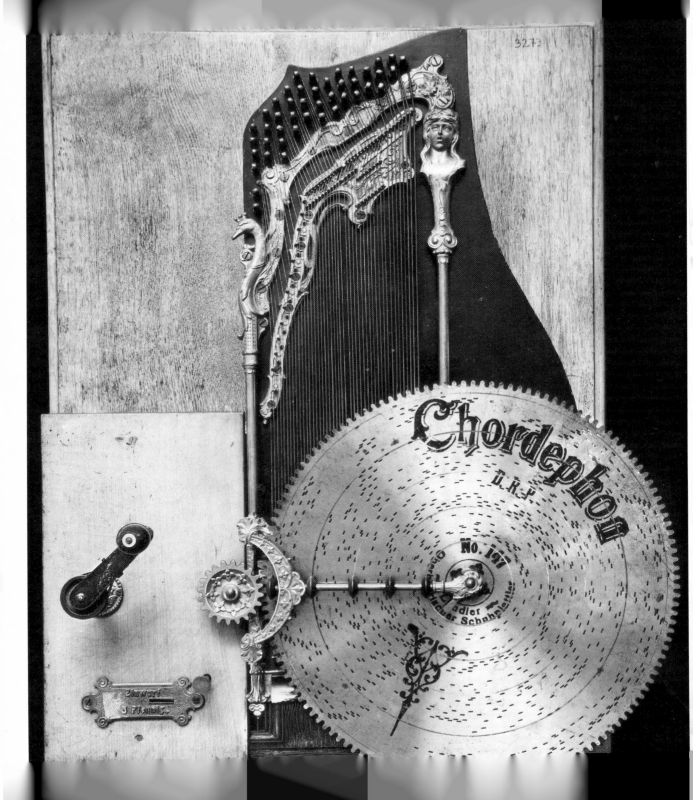

62 Pardessus de viole, Adrien Chatelin, Valenciennes, 1758;
Leipzig, Musikinstrumenten-Museum der Karl-Marx-Universität.

63 Dessus de viole (detail), Louis Guersan, Paris, 1750;
Leipzig, Musikinstrumenten-Museum der Karl-Marx-Universität.

Full-figure Representations of Individuals

We begin this chapter by considering two remarkable keyboard instruments with such a wealth of ornamentation that one hardly notices the individual details: an Italian spinet and the virginal of Catherine of Brandenburg, both instruments completely covered in precious stones.

44 The Italian *spinettino* was built by the famous Milanese (Mediolanensis) craftsman Annibale Rossi in 1577—the label reads: Annibalis de Roxis Mediolanensis mdlxxvii. The Victoria and Albert Museum in London has drawn up a list of the precious and semi-precious stones used on this instrument. It shows that Rossi, whom we can trace back to 1550, used 14 different types of gems:

857 turquoises, 361 pearls, 242 small garnets and rubies, 117 garnets, 103 lapis lazuli, 58 topazes, 52 jaspers, 40 emeralds, 32 sapphires, 28 amethysts, 19 small jaspers and agates, 9 agates, 6 carneoles and 4 rock crystals.

In addition to the magnificent and exquisite ornamentation in Italian late Renaissance style, there is a second point of interest: the boxwood figurines on either side of the keyboard. On the left, a child is hugging the legs of a naked woman, on the right stands a helmeted warrior in classical pose—possibly she represents Aphrodite with Cupid and he Ares.

This *virginal* of Catherine of Brandenburg is steeped 43 in Transylvanian and Hungarian history. In 1626 the sister of the unfortunate George William, Elector of Brandenburg, whose sorry reign lasted from 1619 to 1640 (he was succeeded by the Great Elector), became the second wife of Gabriel (Gábor) Bethlen. He was elected Prince of Transylvania in 1613 and thereafter pursued a very idiosyncratic policy based on opposition to the Holy Roman Emperor. Bethlen developed his country to the best of his ability; among his achievements was the founding of an academy in Alba Regia (today Székesfehérvár), the old royal seat of the Magyars.

Hungarian researchers believe the virginal, built in 1617, was made in the Southern German town of Augsburg, particularly as it is reminiscent of the cases of ebony and ivory marquetry for which that city was famous. It is lavishly covered with partly enamelled and partly gilded pictures on silver plate. The folding panels on the inside surface of the lid depict the four senses, and concealed behind them are four biblical scenes (see below). The outer surfaces, which we cannot see, carry pictures of the four seasons and the seven liberal arts. There are three more plates above the keys: on the middle one, the organ, cello and mandolin are being played and Cupid is keeping time. On the nameboard is a double Latin motto: OMNIS SPIRITVS LAVDET DOMINVM—"Let every living thing praise the Lord"; and SIC TRANSIT GLORIA MUNDI—"Worldly glory is short-lived". The raised lid shows the four senses with Latin labels: from left to right, AUDITUS—hearing; ODOR—smell; SAPOR—taste; and TACTUS—touch. The figures carry corresponding attributes: guitar, flowers, a bowl of fruit and a parrot. Behind these plates are four biblical depictions showing Jesus in the Temple and the Circumcision, a mirror, the Adoration of the Magi with the Shepherds in the centre, and the Annunciation to Mary.

We have already come across the pyramid piano, which was a derivative of the clavicytherium or vertical harpsichord and which was characterised by its symmetrical structure. A much commoner variation on the same theme was the *giraffe piano* which retained the traditional arrangement of the strings whereby the deep, long strings were on the left and the short, treble strings on the right. Christoph Ehrlich, a piano-builder from Bamberg, was known to have produced instruments between 1816 and 1850. He built this giraffe piano cum furniture-piece in pure classical style. The first thing we notice are the two accessories, which have no musical function, but which served to integrate the instrument into the interior decor of the salon. These are the classical bowl above the bass strings and the clock in its symbolic lyre frame above the short treble strings. The case is of polished mahogany with various bronze trimmings. The pillar on the left shows a vine twisting around the thyrsus (a pine cone on a stick) of Bacchus (Dionysus) and in the middle of the thyrsus level with the lyre—Apollo's old instrument—is its diametrical opposite, the Pan-pipe. A second, ornamental lyre can be seen beneath the clock and two groups of figures adorn the nameboard. Two ram's heads decorate the tips of the lyre/clock, while between them is a female sun, which has a larger male equivalent prominently displayed under the keyboard. The raised lid largely obscures the quarter circle above the keyboard which bears a landscape—only a hill with a castle is visible. From there, a number of curved bars fan out. Cloth covers the whole soundboard both above and below the keyboard.

The two angels—or winged Muses?—only appear to support the keyboard. They are dressed in classical manner with the Greek peplos and the girdle below the breast, as popular in classical times as in Ehrlich's day.

Some observers may be surprised to see six pedals instead of the customary two. Three pedals helped to soften the sound. One of these was a damper, which shifted the action. Another was a piano pedal, consisting of a strip of felt. A third acted as a mute for protection or practising. The three remaining pedals imitated instruments. One pedal imitated bells, another a drum by striking a rib of the belly. Another pedal imitated a bassoon by using a parchment slip. It seems to anticipate the "prepared piano" of the composer John Cage.

Among the relatively rare examples of symmetrically constructed upright pianofortes is this *pyramid piano* built by Caspar Schlimbach (1777–1861) in Königshofen near Würzburg in 1825. He was also a renowned organ builder. The instrument depicted is a salon piece and shows an unusual juxtaposition of two groups of figures: on top of the instrument are two natives and below the keyboard are two atlantes. The lower half of the atlantes has been replaced by pillars, except for the feet. In the apex of the soundboard is a large lyre which dominates the whole instrument.

The ease with which classical and Christian motifs were intermingled is again evident on the reverse of this 19th century neo-Baroque *kit* from Bohemia. It clearly depicts an angel carrying King David's heavenly instrument, the harp. This angel, however, is coquettishly showing a shapely leg and, in the right hand, is invitingly holding a laurel wreath, the classical reward for artistic excellence. The tender embrace of the two putti at the bottom must be construed as a vicarious demonstration. In any case the celestial motif is well complemented by earthly sensuality.

On the front of the *kit* or *pochette*, which was a pocket violin used by dancing masters, we can see ivory inlay on the tailpiece showing Cupid with his lute and the chubby face of a girl surmounting the peg-box. On the soundboard, we can also see the typical juxtaposition of normally exclusive sound-holes. Higher up is a double rose and under the bridge are two flame-shaped holes—the typical sound-hole of the viola d'amore.

34 The above observation is confirmed by another *kit* on the reverse of which we can see both the monogram and the full name of its former owner, CONRAD(US) MULLER. In a play on his own name, which means "miller", he had a picture of a miller's mule carrying a sack of flour—or gold?—inscribed on the instrument together with a lovely girl without any clothing. The naked girl has been deliberately placed where the left hand grips the instrument. Dominating the reverse of the peg-box is a scowling devil's face, and on the front, the head of a young man and woman (cp. Plate 52). One would not be wrong in assuming that it was the same girl in each case.

One's enjoyment in contemplating the instrument is somewhat marred by the false date given—1520—whereas this kit was actually made in 1690. Either the owner's vanity or the manufacturer's greed could have been responsible for this forgery.

40 This unsigned and undated *harpsichord* from Venice is comparable to the semi-mechanical "Polyphemus and Galatea" model considered above. The pictorial designs are also familiar to us from earlier chapters. For example, there is the Orpheus theme on the lid or on the sides with their musical amorettes painted in the charming and delicate early French Rococo manner (this was possibly a 19th century addition). On the outside of the lid, a courting couple are shown in a romantic setting.

Our attention is captured by the two putti which replace the front legs (cp. the tritons on "Polyphemus and Galatea"). Forming the third leg is a winding acanthus, with two birds "kissing". They are rooted in a platform which reproduces the outline of the harpsichord. In the middle is a lyre. Since the keyboard is much higher than normal, owing to the two child-sized putti and the platform, it is assumed that it was played from a standing position.

41 Among the instruments of the imaginative Renaissance was the *lira da braccio*. All well-educated and refined Italians at that time were expected to be able to play it—Leonardo da Vinci was said to be a virtuoso—and it was a must, either as a solo instrument or as part of an ensemble, for accompanying recitals of both classical and modern poetry. Thus one should not be surprised

to find the somewhat highbrow Greek inscription on an ivory plate on the reverse of the instrument:

ΛΥΠΗΣ ΙΑΤΡΟΣ ΕΣΤΙΝ ΑΝΘΡΩΠΟΙΣ ΩΔΗ
"Singing is medicine against human suffering".

The instrument shown was built in Verona in 1511 by Giovanni d'Andrea and is the only surviving such instrument by him; indeed very few lira da braccios at all are in existence today. By a strange and ambiguous quirk, the front has been made to resemble a man—the peg-box as a grotesque face and the soundboard as a torso with nipples, waist and thighs. The back, howev- **42** er, has a female form with a smiling face on the peg-box, nipples with clearly rounded breasts and a navel. But that is not all; the wood on the back was thicker and could sustain carvings, so d'Andrea at the same time carved a bearded man's face all down the reverse side of the instrument. The positioning of the geometric pattern and the ivory inscription is indicative of the supreme sensuality and *joie de vivre* of the Renaissance, refined by high intellectual and artistic demands.

Next in this chapter comes one of the few examples of an individually decorated modern piano. Alexandre Charpentier built the *concert grand* shown here in 1902 **45** and Albert Besnard (1849—1934) was responsible for the decoration. This artist of the Art Nouveau school chose to give the elongated instrument, the legs and case of which he himself carved from ebony, an appearance of lightness and almost weightlessness. He accomplished this via the thinness of the convoluted legs, the dispersion of the weight among six legs instead of the usual three, and by the curved struts that connect the front four legs which meet at the lyre assembly. This assembly rises up to the belly like a plant forcing its way up through the earth. Equally as significant and impressive as the structure and, one might say, the dynamism of the form is the artist's pictorial decoration. He may be placed between neo-Impressionism and Symbolism and is known, among other things, for his work on the epoch-making "L'Art Nouveau" salon built for the art dealer Salomon Bing in Paris in 1895, and also by the stained glass window—"Les Paons" (the peacocks)—which he designed for the Musée des Arts Decoratifs.

In line with the old tradition, he devoted the whole of the enormous lid interior surface to a single picture and also decorated the visible sides with a frieze painted in a very plastic style. The large picture on the lid shows a naked woman—a symbol of musical ecstasy—being carried along by a sea of sound, the shimmering waves of which are indicated by threads of gold which sensuously entwine her. The frieze portrays the magic powers of music and the various kinds of enrapturement into which it can transport us—the scale ranges from reverie via adultery to murder! Most vivid of all is the central scene, heavily charged with tension, which is a kind of variation on Tolstoi's "Kreutzer Sonata".

Four musical angels with gilded wings, carved by the sculptor Johann Adam Georgi, brighten up the front of the great *cathedral organ* in Freiberg. This famous creation of Gottfried Silbermann was completed in 1714 One of Georgi's celestial musicians appears to be playing the keyboard of a positive, which is surmounted by real organ pipes. The angel, which is seated casually on a ledge of the organ case, has his head coquettishly thrown back as if following the directions of a conductor.

Perhaps we can take this opportunity to briefly consider the family of Gottfried Silbermann. The first brother, who was five years older than Gottfried, was called Andreas and was born in 1678. They came from the village of Kleinbobritzsch in the Ore Mountains in Saxony. Andreas then moved to Görlitz, where he studied. He spent some time in Alsace before going to the Palatinate and then Paris. He settled in Strasbourg in 1701 and, in the following year, Gottfried became his apprentice. Seven years later, Gottfried returned to Saxony where he undertook as only his second contract the construction of the three-manual organ in Freiberg cathedral. Of his three other triple-manual works, only the one in Dresden cathedral still survives. Double-and single-manual organs built by him are to be found in Freiberg, where there are three including one now in the cathedral, and in Rötha, Bad Lausick, and a few Saxon villages.

Gottfried Silbermann made around 50 instruments. Apart from building organs, he also made a name for himself with his construction of a special clavichord—the "cymbal d'amour"—the strings of which were twice as long as normal thus correspondingly increasing the depth. He also achieved notoriety for his improvements to Cristofori's invention, the pianoforte. The other members of the Silbermann clan—Johann Andreas, Johann Daniel and Johann Heinrich—were all sons of the Andreas Silbermann who lived in Strasbourg. All of them remained in contact with their uncle Gottfried and with Freiberg: J. Andreas went on a study-trip there, J. Heinrich became apprenticed to his uncle, and J. Daniel became his colleague in 1752 and, one year later, his sole heir after Gottfried died.

Carved Heads and Portraits

In this chapter, due attention will at last be paid to the stringed instruments, which lacking large surface areas and in view of certain technical restrictions carried relatively little or normally very modest decoration compared with the keyboard instruments. Even though, as a rule, the carved heads which were characteristic of many of these instruments had only a decorative function, the artists nevertheless often managed to express individual personalities through the facial features of their sculptures.

The first signed violin of the world-famous maker Antonio Stradivari is dated 1665 although it took him until the turn of the century to evolve his unique standard style by which he is known to posterity. Several experts ascribe this *cittern*, made in 1700, to him. It is an early example of the cittern, a plucked descendant of the fiddle, since it has front pegs instead of the later traditional lateral pegs.

The cittern bears three main carvings: a small, naked female figure at the end of the finger-board; a pair of lovers emerging from a torso on the reverse of the instrument; and a strikingly carved woman's head crowning the peg-box, which is featured in the picture. From amid a welter of bizarre ornamentation, an inquisitive face with slightly parted lips and large, alert eyes stretches forward.

This beautifully shaped and finely decorated Bohemian *viola d'amore* made in 1769 is surmounted by a carved Cupid whose eyes are bandaged. Our Plate shows the technical peculiarity of this "love-viol", which had a particularly warm and rich tone. It had between five and seven (as here) melody strings for playing, which ran over the bridge and terminated at the lower end of the peg-box. In addition, it had between seven (as here) and fourteen sympathetic (i. e. freely vibrating) strings, which ran under the bridge and finger-board and were secured to the smaller pegs at the top end of the peg-box. Since the sympathetic strings ran underneath the melody strings, the peg-box was tilted slightly back. Another typical feature of the instrument, which probably first appeared in England around 1650, but had already gone out of fashion by 1800, was the presence of two flame-shaped sound-holes together with a rose (cp. the kit).

Franz Geissenhof built this *viola d'amore* in 1779. It is decorated with a handsome boy's head which, in keeping with the tradition of this instrument, bears a blindfold, and also a kind of collar.

Next comes another *viola d'amore*. It was made by Kaspar Stadler in Munich and is untypical in having a sex-less girl's head carved on the peg-box. It is an example of a decorative and ornamental mask of the type common in the late Baroque era. We shall come back to this instrument later on when we shall deal with the marquetry on the reverse of the body (cp. Plate 101).

58 Two *viola da gambas* crowned with carved female heads present a striking contrast. The first was built by the great Tielke in 1691 and has already been discussed (Pl. 26). On the front, above black marquetry on a white background, is a head carved of ivory representing Artemis. She is wearing a fantastic helmet, which in turn is topped by a grotesque devil's face. One could hardly describe it as beautiful; the forehead is cold and the hairline is covered by the helmet. The face expresses a strange serenity. Its static and symbolic style is in stark 59 contrast to the *alto gamba* built in 1731 by the Leipzig craftsman Johann Christian Hoffmann. Here the carved head, which grows organically from the gently curving peg-box, is powerfully expressive. A series of coincidences connected Hoffmann's life to that of his contemporary Johann Sebastian Bach: he was born just two years before Bach (1683), came to Leipzig one year before him (1722) and died in the same year as the great composer (1750) and in the same place. Rudolf Steglich directly refers to him as "Bach's instrument-maker". In his first year in Leipzig, Bach ordered a viola pomposa from Hoffmann for which he then arranged the last of his Six Suites for Violoncello (Opus 1012, 1720).

Although a highly prized instrument in the Middle 54 Ages, the *hurdy-gurdy* became so despised after 1400 that Michael Praetorius considered it beneath his dignity in his "Organographia" to discuss this "instrument of peasants and women". It then made a fashionable comeback on a wave of nostalgia and sentimentality in 18th century France in the form of the "vielle". It became a lavishly decorated instrument, as we can see from the picture of a hurdy-gurdy built by Levalois in Paris in 1753. We can clearly see the melody strings flanked by two sets of drones. The thickset woman's head garlanded with flowers on the peg-box matched the squat shape of the instrument.

On larger viols and particularly double basses, carved heads often appeared rather small in comparison with the instrument as a whole, but this was never a problem 56 with the *kits*. These miniature, club-shaped instruments provided a fitting torso for a carved woman's head. Our

picture of a 17th century French kit is a perfect example: the gently curving peg-box also serves as the woman's neck, so that the delicate inclination of her head appears a totally natural movement.

This *kit*, made by Conrad Müller, has already been 51 discussed (see Pl. 34). It is unusual in having a finial in the form of two heads. In all probability, the carving represents the musician himself and his young wife or mistress, who is also depicted naked and in the company of two children on the reverse.

Carvings are sometimes found on *basset-horns*, 50 though this was unusual on wind instruments. It was a kind of alto clarinet with a downward extension of the pitch and is said to have been invented by Mayrhofer in Passau in 1770. Like the early cor anglais it was originally a curved instrument, and because of this and its deep pitch was known as the "small bass (basset) horn". Mozart was so taken with its delicate tone that he included it in four compositions (K 361, 410, 411 and 440c) in which he paired it respectively with oboes and clarinets, horns and bassoons. He also included it in the scores of the "Magic Flute" and "Titus". His example was followed by Beethoven, Mendelssohn and then Strauss, who used it in "Elektra" and "Die Frau ohne Schatten".

In the course of time, the curve developed into a crook and the "box" covering this angle was sometimes carved, as in our picture of an 18th century Bohemian basset-horn. In its definitive form, the instrument was more compact and less bulky: either single-reed with an upturned bell, or with a double lower joint like a bassoon.

The *baryton*—our picture shows one made by Daniel 55 Achatius Stadlmann in Vienna in 1732—was, like the lira da braccio, a very exclusive kind of instrument which could only be played by experts, and it was a stiff test even for them. It was never popular and in France completely unknown. Few players were able to produce the full, rich tonal range and colours of the instrument. One of the few was Prince Nikolaus Esterhazy for whom his personal music master, Joseph Haydn, wrote 175 compositions either for or including the baryton. The carved head on the instrument depicted in our picture shows a coarse-featured man with a hat and beard; marquetry covers the finger-board and tailpiece.

Well before Stadlmann was making his barytons, this
61 *tenor viol* was made by Thomas Edlinger the Elder in
Augsburg (1672). It has a finial in the form of a man's
head with a hat and pointed chin. It is a fascinating facial study of an old man, who is clearly moved by
something he has heard. His eyes are raised either in
deep emotion or pious rapture.

Character studies of two young men end this "male
62 section". The *pardessus de viole* made by Adrien Chatelin in 1758 is surmounted by a Turk's head with a curling moustache and turban fixed at the front by a cres-
cent-shaped brooch. Such exotic motifs were very much
in vogue at the time as can be seen from the quasi-Turk-
ish names of a number of Mozart's works: the "Turkish March", "Entführung aus dem Serail", and the
masquerades in "Così fan tutte". This exotic tendency
also included the chinoiseries, a topic which we will
deal with separately.

The name meant "super treble viol" and it was so called because it was a treble viol which lacked the sixth
and deepest string. It was introduced in the 18th century and soon became the favourite instrument of refined French ladies prior to the Revolution. The sixth
63 string was re-included on the *dessus de viole*—our picture shows one made by Louis Guersan of Paris in 1750
surmounted by a young peasant with a mussel-shell
hat—which thus needed an extra peg.

48 This *violin* was made by the Parisian craftsman Jean
Baptiste Vuillaume (1798–1875) and has an interesting
history. In addition to cunning forgers, such as Franciolini (see Pl. 14), there were also officially recognised
imitators. Vuillaume, based in the French capital from
1819 onwards, was one of them. The violin illustrated
was a copy he made of one which the great Italian maker Guarneri had made for Louis XIV. Andrea Guarneri, who died in his native town of Cremona in 1698,
was, like Stradivari, a pupil of Nicola Amati. However,
the name Guarneri is more often associated with his
grandson Guiseppe Antonio (nicknamed "del Gesù")
who is said to have studied under Stradivari. It was also
from him that Paganini got his instrument. Other prominent members of the family were Andrea's sons Pietro (who settled in Mantua) and Guiseppe Giovanni
Battista, who was also influenced by Stradivari, and the

latter's eldest son Pietro (who later moved to Venice),
brother of del Gesù.

On the back of the violin, Guarneri/Vuillaume painted an attractive female portrait on the upper bout; the
face is like the sun breaking through dark clouds. The
complementary picture on the lower bout, which today
(as doubtlessly in Vuillaume's time, too) is only partly
intact, shows a town wall and landscape by night. Separating the two pictures is the motto: JUSTITIA—PIE-
TATE—"Justice from Piety"; it was not a particularly apt
description of Louis XIV's life.

Vuillaume was especially renowned for his copies of
Stradivari violins. He was also a prolific inventor: he
constructed a viola with an extended tonal range, which
he called "contralto" and a huge double bass some four
metres tall ("octobasse"), which was pitched an octave
below the cello. He also made a number of useful inno-
vations in the manufacture of strings and of violin bows.

Although the mechanical instruments which were
mass-produced at the turn of the century lie outside our
terms of reference, we will make an exception in the
case of one which has numerous points of interest for
us. Large numbers of *chordophones* were produced 60
around 1900 by the Leipzig firm Clauss. It was a kind of
mechanical zither: when a coin was dropped into the
slot on the left it released a spring which set the perforat-
ed disc in motion. Small teeth on the disc made contact
with the relevant strings. Its form harks back to that of
the lyre. On the right is a bronze bust depicting a kind
of standardised Muse and on the left we can see a
crowned swan. This is quite apt because the instrument,
whose cast-iron frame in industrial-gothic style is reminiscent of the sewing machines produced at the time
and is a kind of swan song of the individually decorated
musical instrument.

The *pedal-harp* made by Jean Henri Naderman in 57
1785 is something of a prototype of industrial mass-
production. Beneath the curved neck, which is richly
bedecked with acanthus leaves, is a female bust; the ancient Egyptian head-gear lends an exotic air to her symmetrical features. The early classical ornamentation is
typical of the Louis Seize style.

In a church in Arnstadt, a little town in Thuringia, is
a rare example of a musical instrument which bears the

portrait of a composer. Johann Sebastian Bach was seventeen when he heard that the church of St. Boniface in Arnstadt, which was destroyed in a fire in 1581, was being rebuilt and fitted with a new *organ*. He applied for the job of organist and meanwhile got a job as a violinist at the court in Weimar until the building was finished. There he became the "Official Organist to the Prince of Saxony"—a title which he later used to his advantage—and then went to Arnstadt, first to inspect the new organ and a few weeks later to start his new job. The organ was not very big but was quite well made. In his obituary Forkel wrote: "Here he eagerly set about studying all the works of the leading contemporary organists he could find in order to improve his own compositions and the art of organ-playing."

The organ was given its present form and sound in 1913 by a firm from the town of Oetting. The organ case is unchanged from Bach's day, except for the addition of a portrait of him framed by his name and period of service at the church. The original console is today in the Bach Museum in the town. The church now bears the name of its most famous organist and choirmaster.

Landscapes, Buildings and Pillars

In Paris in 1677, the Bolognese craftsman Faby built a 64 *harpsichord* for Count Hercule Pepoli—his coat-of-arms are displayed on the nameboard—which has typically Italian features. The instrument is lavishly decorated, a reflection of the customer's social position (Louis XIV was one of his godfathers).

The decoration includes marquetry of ivory, ebony and mother-of-pearl which extends even to the tops and fronts of the keys. However, the central attraction is the picture on the lid interior, which depicts an idyllic landscape with mountains, lakes and castles populated by several strolling couples.

The hinge separating the front top, which forms part of the picture, from the wing lid has been skilfully placed against a bright background. In turn, the golden skyline and mountain range form a vivid contrast to the azure heavens. As in many other paintings, two trees dominate the perpendicular perspective. They deliberately straddle the joint, their branches covering it above and the trunks distracting attention from it through the contrast of light and shade. The couple at the centre of the foremost section of the picture appear to be a gentleman with one foot raised as if ready to dance and a country girl whose hand he has snatched to kiss it.

The brightness of the background is enhanced by the modest decoration on the sides: the dark blue colouring is offset only by a little imitation marble marquetry. On the nameboard on either side of the coat-of-arms are two cartouches of landscapes of ivory marquetry 65 flanked by two grotesque masks.

Next we see a *harpsichord*, which was built by an un- 72 known Italian craftsman a century or so later. It illustrates the big change in style that occurred during the intervening period. The main features are its classical simplicity and avoidance of superfluous ornamentation and the contrast between the rather vague and dreamlike landscape (prefiguring Böcklin's painting "The Isle of the Dead" of 1883) and the elegant and restrained case of cypress wood. On a grey background (pure white was considered too garish) are a few sparse gilt decorations of flowers. The delicate legs, of which there are only five (the long straight side on the left has no additional support), give an impression of lightness. Ivory and ebony marquetry on the keys and nameboard complement the well-balanced and refined decoration.

Unlike the sloping lid on Faby's instrument, this harpsichord has a vertical front flap. This was a typical feature of Italian harpsichords, which had to fit into an outer case. Consequently the painter was able to use the full length of the instrument for his picture. The painting and its theme of Nature address themselves directly to our emotions.

The next instrument illustrated is absolutely exqui-
71 site. It is a double manual *harpsichord* and was built by
one of the most famous craftsmen of his day (and is the
oldest surviving instrument by him). This instrument
was decorated by first-rate Dutch painters, including
one of that country's very finest artists. In addition, it
has one of the most remarkable histories imaginable.

It was built by Hans (Jean) Ruckers the Younger,
whom we have already mentioned several times, in Antwerp in 1612 and is thus the oldest known of his works.
The two paintings on the lids were the work of Jan
Brueghel the Elder ("Velvet Brueghel"), who died in
1625, Hendrik van Balen (d. 1632), and Paul Bril
(d. 1626). In addition, the soundboard is painted with
garlands of flowers: this was the work of Frans
Francken who died in 1643. We do not know who was
responsible for the paintings on the sides.

Brueghel painted the wing lid, but left van Balen to
do the scene with Apollo and Marsyas (we have already
discussed their contest and its gory outcome). What
particularly interests us here is Bril's picture showing
Orpheus surrounded by the wild beasts. This subject
has already been dealt with in its proper place, so I will
restrict myself to drawing the reader's attention to the
perfect harmony of fauna and flora in the Garden of
Eden.

The instrument has a remarkable history which
touches on a whole galaxy of famous European personalities and monarchs.

Henry IV of France, who even switched religion in
order to unite his country ("Paris is well worth a
mass"), at last managed to establish a period of relative
security and economic prosperity. In 1610, ten years after marrying Marie de Medicis, he took her to the Ab-
bey of St. Denis (where all the French monarchs since
Merovingian times were buried) in order to crown her
as his queen. On the way home, he was murdered. Two
years later his widow ordered the harpsichord illustrated from Ruckers in Antwerp as a present for the king's
eldest daughter Elizabeth, who later married Philip IV
of Spain. Thus the instrument came to the Escorial and
then, after the queen's death, to her daughter Marie
Thérèse, who married the French "Sun-King" in 1660.
She brought the instrument with her to Paris where it

was placed in the salon of her ladies-in-waiting at Ver-
sailles. One of the king's many mistresses—the former
widow of the poet Scarron—eventually triumphed over
her rivals and in 1685, two years after Marie Thérèse's
death, was secretly married to him and given the title of
Marquise de Maintenon. She thus became the new owner of the harpsichord and, after the king died, took it
with her to Saint Cyr where she founded an institute for
impoverished daughters of the aristocracy which she
then ran for the rest of her life.

The *geigenwerk* illustrated in the next picture bears 78
the somewhat misleading inscription "Fra Raymundo
Truchaldo. Inventor. 1625". Although Truchaldo built
this instrument, the idea for the basic motor mechanism
for this piano-violin goes back to Leonardo da Vinci in
1475. Truchaldo designed the four friction wheels onto
which the strings, which were surrounded by wire coils
connected to the jacks, were pulled when the key was
depressed. The handle, which turned the four wheels by
means of a simple transmission mechanism, was worked
by a second person standing behind the instrument—
rather like the early hurdy-gurdies.

The two pictures on the interior surface of the lid of-
fer a stark contrast. The square surface on the left depicts a mythological scene. Two sturdy fish-tailed tritons are abducting a beautiful nude woman who is
vainly trying to avoid being hit by an arrow from Cupid
who is hovering above her. Lust and unrestrained violent force triumph over tenderness and culture. Note
the contrast in colour between the dark sea sprites and
the white skinned young maiden. The dramatic scenery
in the background is a far cry from the neat and sterile
perspective of the adjacent park scene, in which the
fountain provides the watery link with the picture on
the left.

Landscapes can also be considered to include the cur-
rent environment and urban scenes. Another member of
the famous Dutch family of artists, Peter Brueghel the
Elder, who lived from 1525 to 1569, was a competent
chronicler of his time, especially of the life of ordinary
folk.

He is credited with having painted the detailed picture of a Flemish harvest festival ("kermesse") which
adorns a *spinet* made by Hans Grovvelus (Grauwels). 68

94

The picture must have been commissioned independently and added to the lid later after the artist's death.

The picture is teeming with activity. At the centre, just a little to the right, is a large tree which balances the imposing building with a (guild?) flag which looms up in the shade on the left with the group of smaller sunlit buildings on the right. The myriad, bright details form part of a carefully ordered and well-balanced structure: on either side of the tree at the centre of the village green is a line of people. The musical master of ceremonies of this simple folk festival is sitting in the tree and playing the bagpipes.

Hieronymus Albrecht Hass of Hamburg did a solid and technically competent job of constructing this fret-
70 free *clavichord*. It has double courses (i.e. it has two strings per key), which doubles the volume. As an added refinement, Hass put in extra strings for the 22 deepest pairs of strings which were pitched an octave higher, thus giving more precision to the somewhat undifferentiated and muffled tone of the bass strings.

An unusual kind of decoration was employed in order to keep the costs down: a large etching was affixed to the lid. It shows a view of Altona near Hamburg. Such economy measures were commonly employed in the 19th century on musical boxes or other mechanical instruments such as orchestrions, the inner lid being fitted with reproductions of pleasant or sentimental pictures. In addition to the view of the town, the lid carries fashion pictures along the bottom and a cosmopolitan medley of pictures at the sides.

67 The first *square pianos*, which still clung very much to the form of the clavichord, were built by J. Socher from Sonthofen. The instrument shown here was built in 1742 and has three paintings on the inside surface of the lid: Saint Cecilia, the patroness of music, is playing a positive organ as she is dressed in a flowing bright-red robe; she is flanked by scenes of two Italian ports. The artist carefully guides our attention on either side of the central picture past buildings to views of the open sea. Ships painted in some detail are shown at the margins. In the 19th century, the keyboards of square pianos extended across the whole breadth of the instrument; in this form it held its own in England and North America until it was ousted by the pianino—the upright piano.

In the second half of the 17th century (Leopoldo Franciolini was probably responsible for falsely backdating it to 1580; see Pl. 14), an unknown craftsman made an Italian *harpsichord* which carries paintings of the 74 town of Pisa on the two lids. On the wing lid we can see 75 a view of the river Arno, one of the three stone bridges with buildings on them, the old city centre with its famous cathedral and campanile (left), and in the background the Apennines. The river Arno eventually runs into the Ligurian Sea to the west of Pisa. Although the town has been painted with little care, the cathedral which has been painted separately across the front flap is a fairly detailed and accurate picture. On the left is the baptistery, a three-storey building of white marble built in 1278. It is surmounted by a 55 metre high cupola which is crowned by a statue of John the Baptist. Next to it is the main façade of the cathedral with its four tiers of pillars above the portal. This Romanic basilica was completed in 1118 and rebuilt in 1604 after a fire—the artist thus painted a relatively new building. It has five naves and three transepts and at their intersection is a 51 metre high dome. The campanile (bell tower), commonly known as the Leaning Tower, is situated to the east of the cathedral. The camposanto (cemetery), the fourth element of this world famous complex of buildings on the piazza, lies behind the cathedral. There is a memorial there to Galileo—he was born in Pisa but was buried in Florence. It is amusing to note that even in those days people insisted on taking short cuts across the grass!

To round off this section on landscape pictures, we shall examine two extremely intricate works.

On closer inspection, the Italian or Flemish *spinet* 66 made by an unknown master around 1600 proves to be something of a compendium of classical themes. Each of the 18 panels of Murano glass on the inside surface of the lid depicts a landscape in miniature and also bears a label detailing the contents, just like in a museum (with one exception where the label has been lost). The most important scenes, from left to right, show: Daphne, Andromeda, Actaeon, the Triumph of Bacchus(?), Narcissus and Argus; and the bottom row: Thisbe, Pyramus, Artemis, Arcadus and Paris. These colourful glass cameos testify to the outstanding skill of the craftsmen of Murano, a town on the lagoon near Venice which, from the Middle Ages onwards, was the centre of the Venetian glass industry. Let us consider just one of the panels—the one in the middle on the bottom row: it shows Actaeon spying on Artemis as she bathes. The hounds, which will later devour him after she has turned him into a stag, are ready and waiting (third panel from left on the upper row).

The decoration on this instrument is so abundant that it would seem excessive even to the specialist: the ubiquitous five-petalled flower is an annoying distraction both from the music and from the rest of the pictorial decoration.

The instrument once belonged to Elizabeth Stuart, granddaughter of Mary Stuart, who for a short time became the Queen of Bohemia through her husband, the "Winter-King" (see Pl. 28).

73 The second *spinet* was made some 200 years later in Venice, again by an unknown master. Some experts ascribe it to the Venetian Petrus Centamin in view of its resemblance to his works. The instrument and its square case have two kinds of decoration: refined coloured and golden designs on a yellow background, and a total of 16 landscapes spread over its various surfaces. On the outside surface of the lid are three paintings on canvas; the middle one is a melancholy seascape relieved only by a solitary gnarled tree. The other pictures have been painted directly on the case. Floral motifs adorn the inside surface of the lid. In accordance with the yellow background colour of the case, the "white" keys of boxwood also have a yellowish hue. In addition to the two superb paintings showing an arched bridge and a coastal scene on the front flap, the two landscapes which follow the curving contours at the sides also merit our attention.

Columns and pillars—architectural motifs which are often depicted independently of buildings—normally appear on instruments as actual or apparent supports. When the legs of the keyboards were carved in the form of columns, they did indeed bear the weight, but on upright pianofortes and organ cases their function was more a decorative one. On the modern harp the pillar performs a third role—it conceals the steel rods which lead up through the neck to the tuning pins.

Traditionally, carvings or painted floral motifs decorated the base and the top of the pillar on the harp. The most attractive were those which bore a carved female bust at their angular end like some figurehead on an old galleon. Connected to this post or pillar was the shoulder. This often had a winding form and was normally decorated with designs of fruit or flowers. The neck itself tapered down to the soundbox, which ran down to the base of the pillar, growing considerably in width and depth in the process. The soundbox was really the only part of the harp which gave the artist enough space to paint. The rest of the decoration normally consisted of carvings. Modern harps dispense with all ornamentation except for the pillar whose capital and base still carry architectural decoration.

Louis Bonaparte, who for strategic reasons was made King of Holland in 1806 by his older brother Napoleon, soon rebelled against his brother's aggressive policy of exploitation and rapacious foreign policy. He abdicated in 1810 in favour of his son, leaving his wife Hortense to act as regent. The *pianoforte* made for him 69 in 1808 by the firm of "Érard et frères, Paris" today still stands in the royal palace in Amsterdam.

Its well-proportioned form and judiciously placed decor make it a pure example of the Empire style. Its case is mahogany and the legs are carved in the guise of Corinthian columns. The sparse ornamentation includes a medallion bearing the lyre symbol. Gilt animals on a dark-blue background decorate the nameboard, which also displays the maker's name: "Antoine Ascalon fecit 1808".

This requires further comment. Hitherto maker and workshop had usually been synonymous, but now the age of industrial manufacture began with its concomitant division of labour. Although a leading light such as Sébastien Érard could still find time to make inventions, he could no longer build instruments himself—managerial functions claimed his entire energy.

This is an appropriate moment to briefly examine the multi-faceted personality of this man. Even before his revolutionary invention of the double escapement, without which composers like Franz Liszt would not have been able to write such demanding piano pieces, he had been a prominent harp maker and had made a number of original innnovations. Among these was a harpsichord with pedals which could reduce the length of all the strings by half, thus raising the pitch by an octave (1772); the first French piano (1777); and later a two-manual combination of pianoforte and positive organ ("piano organisé"). Érard pianos were owned by the greatest pianists and composers of the day: Beethoven, Hummel, Thalberg, Moscheles, Liszt, Mendelssohn and Verdi.

Four pedals and one knee lever give this instrument additional variations of tone and volume: damper, piano (which inserted a felt pad between the hammer and strings), una corda (the shifting mechanism which corresponds to the left hand pedal on the modern concert grand), lute (which pressed a felt pad against the strings; it continued a tradition that began on the harpsichord), and bassoon (it was worked by the knee lever and was a forerunner of the harmonium swell; like the lute it was a mere strip of paper).

"Music, when soft voices die, vibrates in the memory": this was the title of a painting which incorporated 77 the *giraffe piano* illustrated here. The English artist was also the owner of the instrument. He was William Quiller Orchardson (1835—1919) and he was a contemporary of Dante Gabriel Rossetti, Burne-Jones, Leighton and William Morris who, like him, were all pre-Raffaelites. It is in this style that the instrument, built by the Dutch craftsman Van der Hoef in Amsterdam *c.* 1810, is decorated.

Although it was made during the height of the Empire period, the classical accessories appear strangely unwieldy. The outline is clearly reminiscent of a harp with its pillar, scrolled shoulder and curved neck. Interestingly, the pillar stands separate from the instrument and does not form an integral part of it as in Plate 37. Its Corinthian capital is another reminder of the harp on which floral decoration connected the top of the pillar and the neck. The keyboard rests on two lion supports consisting of a head and one leg. The free-standing pillar served to offset the massivity of the instrument and also added considerably to its width, thereby making for the enormous scroll of the neck.

The start of quasi-industrial production techniques at the beginning of the 19th century led to a quickly expanding market for musical instruments with fierce competition between French, German and English firms. They experimented with many different forms, which today seem rather fanciful. One such curiosity was the *clavi-harp* invented by the German-born maker 76 Johann Christian Dietz in Paris in 1814. This weird experimental combination of keyboard and plucked instrument had only a short-lived existence. Dietz (1769—1845) led a remarkably productive life. His extraordinary inventiveness, which was by no means restricted to musical instruments (in this sphere he specialised in friction instruments similar to the geigenwerk: the "melodion", "trocheon" and "clavi-lyre") brought him to the notice of Napoleon I who summoned him to Paris. After the collapse of the French Empire he moved to Brussels. The strange "clavi-harp"—a combination of piano and harp—was his most important invention in the realm of musical instruments.

Chinoiseries

The next four illustrated keyboard instruments date back to around 1750. It was a period of upheaval, which saw the decline of the Rococo style along with the end of the absolutist monarchies and a revival of anything and everything that was attractive—this also acted as a stimulus to the exotic.

83 Strange contrasts of conception and design mark the decoration of this double-manual *harpsichord* built by Hieronymus Albrecht Hass in 1723. In addition to scenes of a Chinese park and people, there is a somewhat ponderous view of a French garden with mountains in the background. It was based on an Augsburg copperplate engraving and was a theme frequently used in decoration at the time. Delicate sprays of flowers on the side of the instrument form the link between the Baroque painting on the lid interior and the chinoiseries on a bright background which decorate the nameboard, front flap and insides of the panels flanking the keyboards.

Johannes Goermans was a Flemish instrument maker who moved to Paris around 1750 and died there in 1777. Stylistic traces of the Flemish school are visible on

82 the *harpsichord* he made in 1754: on the soundboard with its floral patterns and on the sides (if we disregard the black background), with its designs of musical instruments and flowers.

The contrast with the painting on the lid is even greater this time: against a bright red lacquered background we see a Chinese park and a gazebo with several musicians, though they are playing typically European instruments. The decoration on the sides is rather uninspired but the colour scheme is most fetching: a mixture of lacquered red, gold and black produces an effect both of contrast and warmth.

The instrument has another interesting feature: today it is no longer a harpsichord but a pianoforte. It was converted before 1800 with the jacks becoming dampers. The bare ledge above the keyboard was used to house the second manual.

In 1786, three years before the outbreak of the French Revolution, Pascal Taskin of Paris made a single-manual *harpsichord* which was spared the violent 79 fate which befell the Goermans instrument. It has a Louis Seize stand, but the side walls and the lid, which this time are both decorated à la chinoise, are possibly older. The dark background colour on the sides offers a pleasing contrast to the light finish of the lid. As per usual the pictures, which have been painted with great care, show social scenes set in a miniature watery park landscape. The artist has included as many Chinese artefacts as possible and has deliberately drawn them in a playful, childlike manner. For example, the convex

98

roofs of the pagodas are realistically drawn, but surmounted by European-type towers or turrets. The famous porcelain vases are also depicted, as are mandarins and, in the centre of the front flap, the legendary phoenix—a symbol of good fortune. In depicting bamboo, the artist has somehow managed to turn the pole-like shrub into a winding plant. The artist faithfully reproduces the wonderful rock gardens of the Japanese and Chinese but lets his imagination run away with him and piles the rocks one on top of the other. In portraying musical instruments, he has tried to do justice to the fact that percussion and woodwind instruments play a greater role in the Oriental orchestra. In the centre of the wing lid picture, a mandarin is playing a kind of fiddle while his wife sits next to him with something like a heron perched on her right hand.

81   In 1755 the Hamburg instrument maker Hass, whom we have already discussed, made a fret-free *clavichord* which, with its Oriental decoration, was very much in keeping with the fashion of the time. The stand, which was added later, has a rather cumbersome appearance while the drawer on the right was an expression of the desire to save space. The red colour of the stand harmonises well with the lid painting, which has a yellow background (originally it was probably white). As on the harpsichords of Goermans and Taskin, the dominant colour is red—as indeed it was in most chinoiserie decorations. Possibly this was a reflection of the red lacquered oriental furniture; in Chinese mythology, red was also a symbol of good luck and happiness.

In addition to Naderman and Érard, another firm of harp makers existed in Paris around 1800—Renault et Chatelain—who in 1790 built the *pedal-harp* illustrated. 80 The maker was evidently so proud of the technical innovation that he made the side of the neck out of glass so that the wires connecting the pedals to the tuning pegs were clearly visible. Both sides of the soundbox are decorated with Chinese motifs and at the base, where the soundbox is at its widest and joins up with the pillar, there is again a park scene.

Plants, Animals and Fabulous Creatures

Flowers and Plants

Botanical designs were carved in the three roses of the 103 illustrated *chitarrone* ("large chitarra") or archlute (with a double peg-box because of the many sympathetic strings) by the workshop of Karel B. Dvořak of Bohemia at the end of the 19th century. This instrument was a copy of one made in 1680 by Martin Schlott, a renowned lute-maker in Prague. In the illustration, one can clearly see how the neck tilts to one side to accommodate both the melody strings on the right and the drone strings on the left. It is most interesting to compare the two lower roses, which, though patterned after the same model, are slightly different.

Made by a Southern German craftsman *c.* 1640, this 84 *spinettino* is less than twenty inches long (45 cms. to be exact). It is a combination of miniature virginal and needlework-box—we have already discussed such combination pieces several times—where both lid and base contain a drawer-like compartment. The mirror at the centre of the opened lid was no doubt well appreciated by both musician and seamstress. Since the keyboard of this spinettino is very narrow and the pitch unusually high, many experts assume it was intended for a child or else hardly ever played. The ebony case, in the manner of the Augsburg cases, bears only two types of decorative element: silver ornamentation and engraved medallions. The latter have been made in round, oval and rec-

tangular shape and decorated with floral patterns; even the silver filigree is made to resemble tendrils. The contrast between the dark wood and the light ornamentation is exquisite.

Jean (Jan) Couchet, who joined the Guild of St. Luke in 1642, was the nephew and pupil of Hans Ruckers the Elder of Antwerp and brought the skills he learned to Paris where his customers included the famous Chambonnières. Chambonnières was royal harpsichordist to the Sun-King; his compositions, which were influenced by the music of English virginal players and Spanish harpsichordists (Cabezón), are the oldest remaining works of the French "clavicinistes" of whom he was the chief exponent and doyen. The double-manual *harp-* 87 *sichord* illustrated has three strings per note and was made in 1650, as we can see from the inscription on the nameboard above the second keyboard.

The instrument exudes the Baroque spirit of Louis XIV's court. Floral motifs are ubiquitous: the dark tendrils on a gold background on the insides of the walls; the colourful bouquets, cornucopia and acanthus designs on the gold-coloured outside walls with their subdued grey borders; the seven legs (the narrow end of the instrument is supported by only one leg) all original and decorated with sculptured leaves; and the understretcher, whose natural curves connect the legs togeth-

Previous page:
64 Harpsichord, Faby (Bologna), Paris, 1677;
Paris, Musée Instrumental du Conservatoire.

65 Harpsichord (detail), Faby (Bologna), Paris, 1677;
Paris, Musée Instrumental du Conservatoire.

66 Spinet, Flemish or Italian, *c.* 1600; London, Victoria and Albert Museum.

Double page overleaf:
67 Square piano, J. Socher, Sonthofen, 1742; Nuremberg, Germanisches Nationalmuseum.

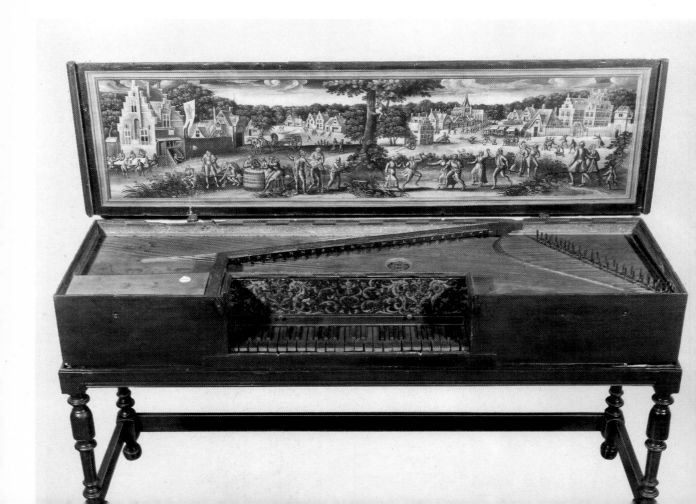

70 Clavichord, Hieronymus Albrecht Hass, Hamburg, 1744; Brussels,
Institut Royal du Patrimoine Artistique.

71 Double manual harpsichord, Hans (Jean) Ruckers the Younger, Antwerp, 1612;
Paris, Musée Instrumental du Conservatoire.

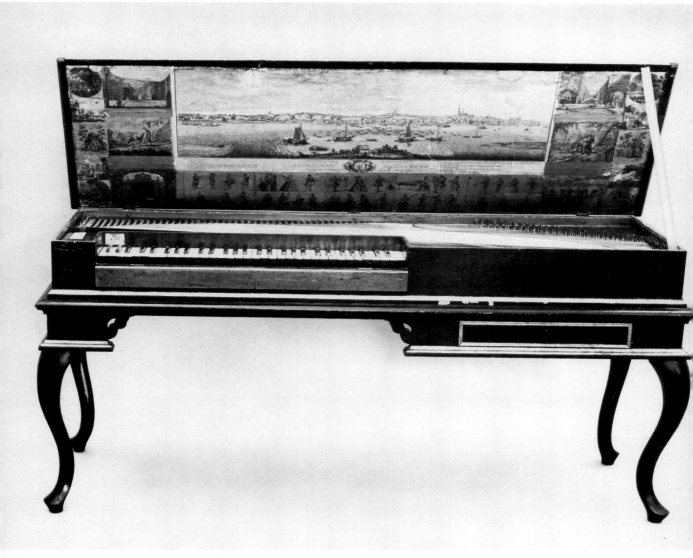

72 Harpsichord, Italian, late 18th century; Hamburg,
Museum für Hamburgische Geschichte.

73 Spinet, Venice, first half of the 18th century; Copenhagen, Musikhistorisk Museum.

74/75 Harpsichord with detail, Italian, second half of the 17th century;
Leipzig, Musikinstrumenten-Museum der Karl-Marx-Universität.

Overleaf:
76 Clavi-harp, Johann Christian Dietz, Paris, 1821;
Leipzig, Musikinstrumenten-Museum der Karl-Marx-Universität.

77 Giraffe piano, Van der Hoef, Amsterdam, c. 1810;
London, Victoria and Albert Museum.

78 Geigenwerk, Raymundo Truchaldo, Italian, 1625; Brussels, Institut Royal du Patrimoine Artistique.

79 Harpsichord (detail), Pascal Taskin, Paris, 1786; London, Victoria and Albert Museum.

Overleaf:
80 Pedal-harp (detail), Renault et Chatelain, Paris, 1790;
Leipzig, Musikinstrumenten-Museum der Karl-Marx-Universität.

81 Clavichord, Hieronymus Albrecht Hass, Hamburg, 1755;
Copenhagen, Musikhistorisk Museum.

82 Harpsichord (detail), Johannes Goermans, Paris, 1754;
New York, Metropolitan Museum of Art.

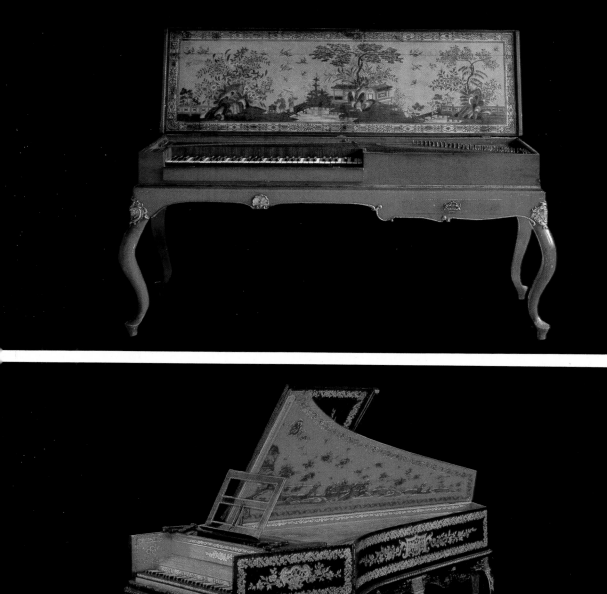

83 Double manual harpsichord, Hieronymus Albrecht Hass, Hamburg, 1723;
Copenhagen, Musikhistorisk Museum.

er and which bears at its centre a carved basket of fruit. Such an abundance of floral and botanical designs comprising flowers, leaves and fruit will not be met with again until the advent of Art Nouveau, which was known in Italian as the "stile floreale".

Flowers and foliage form the decoration of this 17th
92 century Italian *spinet* which evidently must have belonged to a member of the House of Orléans in view of the coat-of-arms beneath the keyboard displayed between two putti. Judging by the height of the instrument, which rests on a symmetrical acanthus frame, it was played from a standing position. An amber medallion with a landscape scene has been set into the nameboard. Apart from two more putti on the inside surface of the lid, all the rest of the decoration is floral.

Louis XIV granted a twenty year patent to Jean Marius of Paris, who is known to have produced instruments at least between 1700 and 1715, for the *folding*
88 *harpsichord* he designed in 1713. For this reason, he stamped all three wrest planks with the inscription "Ex-clusif Privilege du Roy". The idea of a portable harpsichord was prompted by the existence of travelling virginals or spinets and especially by the much lighter portable clavichord.

The wing-shaped instrument is divided into three sections of approximately equal width; the treble end could be rotated about its axis and slotted in beside the central section, reducing the instrument to two equal rectangles. The keyboards were then pushed into the body and the two-section rectangle was folded over onto the bass section. It then measured 140 cms. by 30 cms. by 26 cms. and thus was ready for trans-porting.

In view of the particular nature of the instrument, Marius understandably had to restrict the decoration to the three parts of the soundboard, which is painted with a refreshingly naturalistic collection of loosely scattered flowers with beautiful blossoms, fruit and insects in 17th century Flemish fashion.

98 This fine, single-manual Italian *harpsichord* bears a false label naming Dominicus Pisaurensis (who was active between 1553 and 1575) as the maker, but was in fact built about one hundred years after Couchet's comparable instrument made in 1650 (see Pl. 87). It has a

light and delicate appearance, typical of the Rococo style whereas Couchet's instrument is representative of the more ostentatious Baroque. This harpsichord seems almost weightless; its maker deliberately gave it only five legs (the bent side has an extra support) and their attractive curves make us forget their function. The straight skirting on the underside of the case has been modishly converted into gentle wavy lines which merge naturally into the curves of the legs. For the frames which enclose the delightful bouquets, the artist has chosen an enchanting asymmetrical solution in preference to geometric exactitude. There are a total of ten large floral frames on the outside of the lid and on the sides, all with a light background and gold trimming as if the flowers were embedded in clouds. The spaces in between as well as the stand and legs are painted red, in this way offering a vivid and powerful colour contrast.

Jean Couchet's instrument, particularly the stand, still bears stylistic traces of the Renaissance: no attempt to disguise the function of the legs; a symmetrical and rectilinear structure; an expression of massiveness and solidity (also a large number of legs). This Rococo instrument, in contrast, moves away from ornamentation and towards refined simplicity, thus smoothing the path to the neo-Classicism of the Empire.

By the time the great Sébastien Érard died in 1831, his firm's production range comprised harpsichords, harps, horizontal pianofortes as well as their first upright equivalents, i.e. the modern piano. The *piano* il- 106 lustrated left the firm of Érard in 1834 and according to an entry in the firm's books was delivered by Pierre Érard, who managed the firm at the time, to his brother-in-law Gasparo Spontini who had married Pierre's sister in 1811.

This upright pianoforte, which was still something of a novelty at that time, has the classic shape of the modern piano, though if anything it stands even lower than today's instruments. The case is of elm inlaid with marquetry of mahogany and rosewood in the style of Roman fresco painting and reminiscent of Pompeii: Grecian palm leaves, a frieze of laurel leaves, Etruscan vases and stylised musical instruments. Centrally placed, as on the giraffe pianos, is the obligatory lyre.

Spontini had a long and adventurous life. He ran away both from his family and from the conservatoire, married into the Érard empire and became a partner, served as conductor *(kapellmeister)* to three monarchs—to the Empress Josephine, Louis XVIII and, from 1820, to Frederick William III of Prussia who made him "General Director", a post which was created specially for him. In 1841 following vehement protests by the Berlin public against the "Italian Music Pope", he was forced to resign and to retire to his native village where he died in 1851.

In 1786, only nine years after he made his and France's first pianoforte, Sébastien Érard founded a branch of his firm in London. It was here at roughly the same time as Spontini's instrument *(c. 1840)* that the 94 *grand pianoforte*—better known today as a concert grand—was made. Its sumptuous ornamentation was a product of the first wave of neo-Baroque that swept France after 1830, where it was known as the "deuxième rococo" before spreading to Britain. The instrument is clearly a child of the famous French parent company. The rich marquetry showing landscapes, floral motifs, grotesques and musical instruments is of coloured woods, mother-of-pearl and ivory. It was designed and carved by George Henry Blake. The entire instrument is bedecked with carved scrolls and marked by sweeping curves, including, as on Couchet's instrument, the understretcher, which connects the legs with their exaggerated concave contours to the lyre assembly. The assembly bears the obligatory lyre design but only as a miniature intarsia and not in the traditional carved form. The understretcher is also joined to the two (modern grand pianos normally have only one) rear legs which, like the two front legs, appear to gravitate towards one another and are joined to the understretcher two-thirds of the way down. The rest of the ornamentation consists of carved female heads at the top of the legs, a strange face with puffed cheeks on the lyre assembly and a statue of Apollo beneath the case. He is sitting on a lion's head, another reference to the old dualism: his disciplined musicianship conquers brutality, unbridled power and brute force.

One could hardly expect marquetry to be employed to cover large surfaces on musical instruments or to depict whole scenes. Nevertheless, the next illustration shows a remarkable instrument which is extensively and richly inlaid with marquetry of coloured woods depicting floral designs and other ornamentation. It is a *pyramid piano* made by Christian Ernst Friederici 91 (1709—1780) and is the oldest such instrument still in existence. It was a prototype and is over seven feet high; on later models the height was reduced.

Next come two illustrations of stringed instruments to show that floral motifs were by no means restricted to the large keyboards.

We have already come across one of them: it is the *cello* made for the Duke of Parma-Modena. The back is 96 carved with reliefs showing historical scenes (cp. Pl. 6). The front is profusely painted (carving on the belly would jeopardise the resonance and tonality) with curling plant patterns. The upper and lower bouts each display an heraldic device: the tailpiece is crowded with carved figures, flags and the proprietor's arms (the cross-bearer at the bottom indicated the significance that the feud with the Anglican state church had for James II and the English Catholics); on the other side of the bridge is a double-headed eagle bearing a heart.

The second instrument is a *viola da gamba* and was 85 made by the well-known London craftsman John Rose (or Ross), probably in the middle of the 16th century for the Beauforts, a family of French descent which played an important role in English history. The most famous and successful member of the family was Henry de Beaufort; he was English Chancellor, Envoy to the Council of Constance, a cardinal and a member of the court which sentenced Joan of Arc to be burned at the stake in 1431.

Below the bridge is the customer's brightly painted coat-of-arms bordered by scrollwork. The brown "mauresques" which decorate the whole of the belly are similar to the designs on the previous instrument though the shape and sound-holes of this viol are clearly different: the outline bears several indentations and tapers towards the neck and the flamed F-holes mirror the bizarre shape of the body. The viola da gamba was held between the knees; at this point the indentations turn back in on themselves. In keeping with most viols, this one has a carved female head surmounting the peg-box, though here the eyes are untypically turned towards the right.

Although commonly found among wind and keyboard instruments (aulos, bagpipes, two- or three-manual organs and harpsichords, double virginals) it is very unusual to come across an example of a double instrument among the strings. This French *double guitar* 86 of 1690 is a combination of two guitars with different pitches, one of which seems to grow out of the side of the other. Each part of this extremely rare instrument is decorated with a sunken rose with a trefoil design and two scrolls at the sides of the string-holder.

Animals and Fabulous Creatures

We shall first meet a "menagerie" consisting of goats, birds, lions, horses, dogs and dolphins before going on to look at a varied assortment of fabulous creatures.

104 The *bagpipe* (our picture shows an 18th century German version: a bock with bellows) originated as an animal bladder or skin which had two or three reed-pipes inserted into the natural openings. The player blew through the mouthpipe, which had a valve inside to prevent the air from coming back out again, thus inflating the windsack; the air escaped via the chanter which was fitted with finger-holes to allow the player to alter the length of the vibrating column of air (i. e. the pitch). Soon a third pipe (the drone) was added but because it had no finger-holes the air escaping through it produced a continuous drone. It was therefore suitable for two-part or polyphonic music as were the stringed instruments of the Renaissance with their melody plus sympathetic or drone strings.

By 1600, the bagpipes in Ireland and Central Europe had been fitted with bellows which obviated the need for blowing. This was followed by the appearance in Germany in the 17th century of a "bock with bellows" The German word "bock" means ram or goat and this instrument underlined the connection between the bagpipes and the classical half man/half goat figures (Pan and Marsyas): as a rule the animal's dark fell was left on the bellows and the chanter emerged from the mouth of a very realistically carved head of a goat to which glass eyes were sometimes added. The instrument in the picture also has two natural horns serving as the upturned bells of the two pipes.

One of the many anomalies of musical history is the fact that late-Gothic reliefs show bagpipes in the hands of angels! The Rococo also produced an aristocratic version which was used in the mock-rustic salon charades; some French musettes had ivory pipes and silkcovered bellows (cp. the hurdy-gurdy, which also crossed the boundaries of social class). However, the natural habitat of the bock and bellows was, of course, the market place, weddings and dances—indeed, it can still be found there today in rural areas of the Balkans. The bock is another descendant of the aulos.

Animals were rarely depicted on stringed instruments except as heads on cellos and double basses. The enormous *double bass* illustrated next was made by Gottfried 90 Thielcke in Brescia in 1662, according to the inscription on the back. The end of the instrument is decorated with an impressive lion's head with open jaws and a 89 clearly visible tongue. The belly of this handsome instrument is covered with the written and carved names of former owners and players.

Another *double bass*, built by Giovanni Battista Dini 107 in Lucignano in 1707, has an unusual carving on the peg-box: a parrot-like bird whose feathers reach right down among the tuning pegs. It looks realistic with its glass eyes and open beak with a forked tongue inside, and also the green colouring with which the head and whole instrument are, or were, covered (only a fragment still remains).

A bird also adorns the pillar of the splendidly decorated *pedal-harp* built by Jean Henri Naderman the Eld- 93 er. After Érard, he was the most well-known harp maker in Paris for Marie Antoinette, the last French queen before the Revolution. According to contemporary reports, she was a skilled performer on the instrument. The harp is covered in gilt. Perched amid foliage beneath the scroll of the neck is an eagle, no less. It offers an imperious contrast at the base of the pillar to a group of putti, which are riding sea-horses and blowing trumpets made of mussel-shells. At the base of the soundbox is a park scene with dolphin fountains on either side of the strings.

99   Two dolphins adorn the lyre assembly of a *pianoforte* made in 1810. They form the two arms of the lyre. Separating Marie Antoinette's harp and this grand piano built by Louis Dulcken, who was born in Amsterdam but worked at the Electoral court in Munich, was a revolution and a complete change of decorative style. The modest simplicity, absence of superfluous ornamentation and economical decoration of the stand were all characteristic of the neo-Classical ideal. The case is of mahogany and does full justice to that elegant wood, with merely a border of marquetry around the sides and the inlay on the nameboard.

Empire craftsmen preferred to taper the legs of stringed keyboard instruments which were often surmounted, as here, by an atlas. The gently curving struts which connect the front legs, pedals and lyre assembly appear fresh and vital and form an organic part of the whole structure.

101   We have already discussed the *viola d'amore* made by Kaspar Stadler in Munich in 1714 (cp. Pl. 51) because of its finely carved female head. The back of the instrument is equally interesting. White inlaid designs of grotesques, musicians and a dog cover the entire surface of the dark back and ribs. The dog in this design is dancing sulkily on a table between two female musicians while holding a small branch. In order to show off the figures, which are encrusted partly in silver and partly in brass, Stadler left a space above them. The small grotesque figures and torsoes depict fabulous creatures. In the top left hand corner, we see King David with devilish horns and on the right a harlequin in the manner of Callot; between them is a creature with the attractive face and torso of a girl but with the horrid hind legs of a lion—a sphinx. Two caryatid-like half-figures bear the feet of the two lady musicians on their headgear, their bodies seeming to grow directly out of the foliage. Between them, a menacing hermaphrodite figure with the bearded face of a man and a woman's breasts is blowing on a stylised ornamental double-reed instrument right into the ears of a plant-woman—yet again our old friend, the aulos!

Until the ninth century, only buffalo and bison horns were known in medieval Germany. The first horns made from elephant tusks came to Western Europe from the Byzantine Empire—like the organ—and were known as *oliphants* or "horns of Roland". They were   100 highly treasured by the knights, who valued them as much as their swords.

While the viol described above had some connections with an unreal fantasy world in view of some of its pictorial representation, the history of the oliphant takes us back to the realm of legend. The figure of Roland/Orlando/Ruotland is mentioned in only one source—Einhard's "Vita Caroli Magni" (Life of Charles the Great)—and so his existence is questionable, but Einhard's references were so dramatic that they inspired many a writer. From Spain where he just defeated the Moors, Charles the Great was recalled to Saxony to deal with fresh revolts while Roland, his nephew and Margrave of Brittany, was in charge of the rear. Roland was attacked by Basques and in dead panic blew his horn so fiercely that the veins in his neck burst; King Charles (he did not become emperor until 800) heard his call for help.

The oliphant in the picture bears decorous ivory carvings with scenes of four-horse chariot races and proud lions.

We have already come across examples of fabulous creatures in earlier contexts. Here we shall deal with those beings that consist either of realistic but heterogeneous components or which are entirely imaginary.

It was unusual for heads carved on wind instruments to be attractive or pleasant—unlike those on the viols; in fact, the heads on wind instruments were not even human—this was the saving grace of those on barytons—they were a phantasmagoria of monsters and (at least in Christian terminology) eternally damned creatures of the nether world. Possibly the deep-seeded prejudice against the sensuous wind instruments inherited from antiquity was partly responsible for this.

The two creatures on the illustrated German *record*- 108 *ers* (c. 1730) seem to find the sound which they themselves have produced unbearable. The one on the left appears to be gagged but its bulging eyes show this frog-like monster's horror at the sweet music which is issuing from the fissure below it; the other is gazing upwards with a pained expression on its face, which is partly covered with leaves.

The predilection for carving symbolic animal heads on musical instruments goes back to the Renaissance, the most imaginative artistic period in Europe with the exception of the Middle Ages. But even in the 19th century, there were examples of *tenor trombones* in military bands which had a winding, snake-like shape and a bell in the form of a menacing pair of wide-open jaws (cp. Baroque gargoyles), with occasionally a vibrating tongue as well. Such instruments are vaguely reminiscent of the carnyx, the Celtic military horn which also terminated in a terrifying animal's head.

Via the famous Ambras Collection in the Tirol, word reached Vienna of the most unusual instrument that was ever made. The five *tartolds* (etymology uncertain) represent the extreme of demonic misanthropy and are a combination of dragon's heads and snake bodies. It is supposed that they were used in conjunction with allegorical plays, which were popular and common during the Renaissance as symbols of the nether regions or of mortal peril. Their frightening appearance is exacerbated by the glaring colour of the brass cases. The ensemble is ingeniously constructed and still perfectly playable. Concealed inside the cases are a set of double-reed instruments with coiled piping (something like the modern bassoon). The mouthpiece is here the "tailpiece" from where the pipe, following a double twist, enters the creature's body, spiralling nine or ten times in the process, before emerging in the open mouth where it is concealed by an iron tongue which vibrates as the air passes. The various sizes of the five "dragons" relate to the different pitches: first and second soprano, alto, tenor and bass.

We are in much more amiable company with the figures on the deeply carved relief on the back of the Duke of Parma-Modena's *violin* made in 1687. We have mentioned this several times before. In places, the wood has been completely carved through, and in two places, we can even see daylight through the F-holes on the soundboard! The main items of ornamentation are the two medallions showing the duke's coat-of-arms and a boy fiddler and the boy in the centre flanked by two putti who are blowing pipes. Dominating both sides of the lower bout are two satyrs sitting on plants and skilfully propped up by their hoofs (devil's feet). They are evidently relishing the grapes they are eating. The muscular satyr on the left has his back turned, while the one on the right is looking towards us and contentedly licking his lips. Surveying the whole scene from the base of the peg-box is a typical Renaissance mask in the form of the face of an old man with hair and beard made of leaves.

The most common female creatures were nereids and sphinxes, two of which flank the *lyre-harp* in our picture which dates from the first half of the 19th century. It was made by the Italian Carlo Scalfi, as the two conspicuous labels remind us. Like the lyre-guitar, it was a later equivalent of the classical lyre/kithara and was a fashionable neo-classical instrument often used as a mere theatrical prop. The typical lyre arms serve no real function since nearly all the strings are secured to the body of the soundboard with the exception of the six bass strings (the instrument is entirely double strung). Like the rest of the 32 courses, the bass strings begin at the lower bridge but they run right up to the top of the right arm where the peg-disc is decorated with a crescent; the sun shines down symbolically upon the treble strings—the bass strings clearly represent darkness and night. In contrast to the harsh straight diagonal formed by the wrest-plank, the three slightly curved bridges on the bottom half of the soundboard break up the harsh geometry. Across the surface of the belly as it expands to the right between wrest-plank and bridges, Scalfi carved three roses in ascending order of magnitude. In spite of the exuberant abundance of painting, marquetry and bronze reliefs, there is no doubt that the instrument was actually played by experienced musicians: the proof of this is the fact that the instrument can be easily lifted out of its resting position, and by the presence of an ingenious mechanism which, as on the pedal-harp, raises the pitch of all the strings by a semi-tone.

A crowned nereid with one hand on a pillar—this was the trademark of the Colonnas, an aristocratic family in Rome which we can trace back to 1101 and which exerted a significant influence on church and state affairs and on papal elections. The family produced Pope Martin V (cp. the family history of the Beauforts), many illustrious cardinals, generals, statesmen and scholars. On the *harpsichord* illustrated next, which was made in the middle of the 17th century, the half-sized frame of a beautiful, if somewhat sturdy, nereid fills up the space between the front legs so that the instrument could only be played from a standing position, and even then there was no room for the player's feet or knees.

The mermaid is perched on a strut connecting the two front legs which, like the rear leg, are carved in the form of pillars; her double fish-tail is wrapped round the plank. In the usual Italian manner, the three gilt legs support a decorated outer case within which lies the instrument proper. Of the two paintings on the inside surface of the lid (the artist was probably Gaspard Dughet who died in 1675), the one on the right has a secular theme while the one on the front flap shows a religious scene. Duck-hunting forms the subject matter of the larger picture; the smaller painting has a similar landscape but depicts Tobias, the hero of the Book in the Apocrypha which bears the same name. He is fishing and no doubt about to catch that giant fish that will cause him to utter the famous words: "My Lord, it will eat me!" Behind him stands the angel Raphael who, having passed himself off to both Tobias and his parents as a normal mortal and unselfish friend, will lead him safely through all perils. Between the angels and whale above and the captivating water nymph below, there is a further tribute to classical antiquity in the form of two satyrs bearing baskets of fruit at either end of the keyboard. Amid this classical, fantastic and biblical context, such a mundane occupation as duck-shooting strikes us as refreshingly modern. The combination of everyday 17th century life, biblical history, classical mythology and risqué folk legend combine with Graeco-Roman architecture to provide a bizarre ornamental complex for this sonorous triple-strung harpsichord.

Historical Survey of Musical Instruments

It has become traditional to classify European musical instruments according to how the sound is produced, i. e. depending on whether the instrument is bowed, plucked, blown or struck. The drawback of this method is that it does not allow us to precisely define the instruments, especially as far as the broad spectrum of the stringed instruments is concerned. For this reason, we have opted for the following system of classification under four headings as laid down by Curt Sachs and E. M. Hornbostel in 1914 and incorporating Mahillon's system of 1880. According to this method, the instruments are categorised as chordophones, aerophones, membranophones and idiophones depending on whether the sound is produced by the vibration of a string (Greek chordé), a column of air (Greek aér), a membrane or the body of the instrument itself (Greek idios = self). European instruments largely consist of the first two groups. We shall consider the chordophones in some detail since they are of particular relevance to us.

Aerophones are based on the effect of the lips and tongue on a vibrating column of air—the human voice works on the same principle. Here we distinguish between flutes, reed instruments, the trumpet family and the organ. Human or animal whistling represents the simplest form of this method of producing sound: the

exhaled stream of air is pushed through the natural fissure of the compressed lips against a firm surface—the front teeth—thus creating a vibrating column of air. *End-blown* and *transverse flutes* use the human lips as the required fissure while *recorders* are fitted with a special flue.

The second group operates via reeds which are set in vibration by the stream of air exhaled by the player and in turn cause the column of air to vibrate. Again there are two variants: single-reed instruments such as *clarinets* and *saxophones* (which belong to the woodwinds despite their largely metal construction), and double-reed woodwind instruments, which include the ancient *aulos* (which had a "mouthpiece" and two pipes), the Renaissance *shawm* and, among the modern woodwinds, the *oboe* and the *bassoon*.

The trumpet family largely overlaps with the more common concept of brass instruments. They all operate on the same principle: the air is caused to vibrate by the more or less compressed lips of the player; the mouthpiece serves only to support the lips and the valves extend the tonal range. The two variants can be distinguished at a glance: the curved or looped *horns*, including *bugles* and *French horns*, and the straight *trumpets* (which originally consisted of a single tube), and the relatively modern *trombones*.

The last sub-section comprises the *organ*: a non-stringed keyboard instrument with flue-pipes and reed-pipes (flue and reed instruments) and their direct relatives which are the *positive* (initially only flutes), the *regal* (originally only reeds), the *portative*, the *barrel-organ* and *claviorganum*, and the indirectly related *harmonium* (exclusively reeds) with its folk forms: the *accordion* and the *mouth organ*.

The two categories of instruments which are the least interesting for us may either possess a definite or an "indefinite" pitch. On *membranophones* it is usually a taut animal skin which is caused to vibrate. Drums have an indefinite pitch and timpani definite and variable pitches. Like drums, *idiophones* date back to the beginning of musical history. Here the material of the instrument, such as wood (xylophones, rattles and castanets), metal (bells and gongs) or glass (glass harmonicas) is struck directly and no additional aids such as strings, columns of air or membranes are needed to produce the sound. A fine example of an entire orchestra consisting of idiophones is gamelan music on Bali (Indonesia) whose exotic charm captivated Debussy.

The *chordophones* stimulated the imagination of their makers. They are the stringed keyboard instruments and the many and varied bowed and plucked instruments.

They all have a vibrating taut string to which was added at an early date a soundbox (resonating body). Originally the strings were made of vegetable fibre, later of twisted animal gut and wire (initially brass, from the beginning of the 18th century also iron, from 1834 steel; silver was also experimented with; and nowadays Perlon). In primitive societies, natural soundboxes (e. g. coconut shells or tortoise shells) or carved wooden bowls were used. These were soon replaced by separate wooden ribs glued together to increase their resonance. The first instance of such a soundbox in Europe was the lyre; since then we have come to differentiate between the belly, back and ribs (sides). We further distinguish between those instruments with a stringholder (to which the lower ends of the strings are attached), fastened to the lower rib or lowest point of the body (instruments with an inferior stringholder, such as violins) and those where it is attached somewhere on the soundboard (instruments with a frontal stringholder, such as the guitar). In Europe the strings are mostly held taut by pegs or screws which are called frontal, rear or lateral (such as on all violins) depending on where they are fixed. In view of such "directional" nomenclature, it has proved useful in the case of the compound chordophones (see below) to think of the whole instrument in terms of a living organism and so to refer to the "directions" of the strings; this analogy between bowed or plucked stringed instruments and the human body is quite natural.

We distinguish between two groups of chordophones: simple chordophones (I) whose soundbox exists independently and can be separated from the strings without really jeopardising the instrument's ability to function, and compound chordophones (II). The simple chordophones (I) are also known as zithers (Greek kithára, Latin cithara) and comprise two sub-groups depending on the type of soundboard: the bar zithers which were exclusively folk instruments (I1) and the board zithers (I2), either with a finger-board (I21) or without. Those with a finger-board included the *lyre-shaped zither* of the Empire and the usually heart-shaped *bow zither*. Eventually, those zithers without a finger-board (I22) were to triumph, though here again we must differentiate between those equipped with keys (Latin clavis) and those without. The earliest forms had no keyboard (I221)—e. g. the *harp-zither*, and the *psaltery*, which formed the basis for all later harpsichords and pianofortes in the broadest sense (Greek psallein = to pluck). It probably hailed from the Orient and soon established itself in Europe (one appeared carved in relief in 1184). Later it fell into social discredit (it was mentioned in 1589 as a carnival instrument) before returning to fashion in the 17th and 18th centuries in the form of the dulcimer. However, in the realm of serious music, the group of zithers with keys but without a finger-board (I222) was paramount. This group is also of exceptional importance as far as pictorial decoration is concerned. According to the method of sound production, we differentiate here between the sub-groups clavichords, harpsichords (including the spinet/virginal), pianofortes and piano-violins.

84 Spinettino, South German, *c. 1640*; London, Victoria and Albert Museum.

85　Viola da gamba, John Rose (Ross), London, probably mid-16th century;
Oxford, Ashmolean Museum.

86　Double guitar, Alexandre Voboam, Paris, 1690; Vienna, Kunsthistorisches Museum.

87　Double manual harpsichord, Jean (Jan) Couchet, Paris, 1650;
New York, Metropolitan Museum of Art.

88 Folding harpsichord, Jean Marius, Paris, 1713; Leipzig, Musikinstrumenten-Museum der Karl-Marx-Universität.

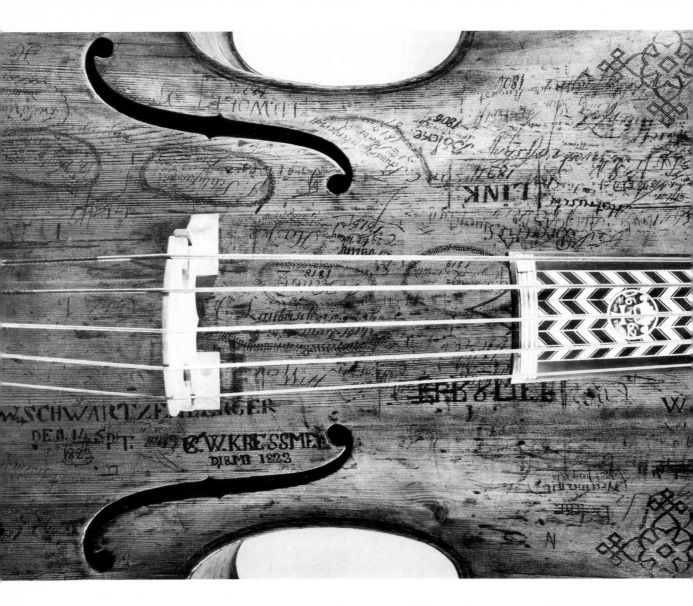

89/90 Double bass (details), Gottfried Thielcke, Brescia, 1662;
Leipzig, Musikinstrumenten-Museum der Karl-Marx-Universität.

Overleaf:
91 Pyramid piano, Christian Ernst Friederici, Gera, 1745;
Brussels, Institut Royal du Patrimoine Artistique.

Previous page:
92 Spinet, Italian, 17th century; Paris, Musée Instrumental du Conservatoire.

93 Pedal-harp (detail), Jean Henri Naderman, Paris, 18th century;
Paris, Musée Instrumental du Conservatoire.

94 Grand pianoforte (concert grand), Érard, London, c. 1840;
New York, Metropolitan Museum of Art.

95   Violin, Domenico Galli, Parma, 1687;
      Modena, Galleria Estense.

96   Cello, Domenico Galli, Parma, 1691;
      Modena, Galleria Estense.

97 Harpsichord, Italian, mid-17th century; New York, Metropolitan Museum of Art.
98 Harpsichord, Italian, mid-18th century; Copenhagen, Musikhistorisk Museum.

99   Pianoforte, Louis Dulcken, Munich, 1810;
Nuremberg, Germanisches Nationalmuseum.

100 Oliphant, before 778; Prague, Treasure of St. Vitus' Cathedral.

Following pages:

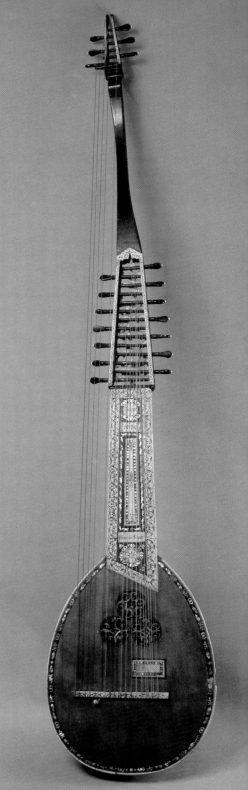

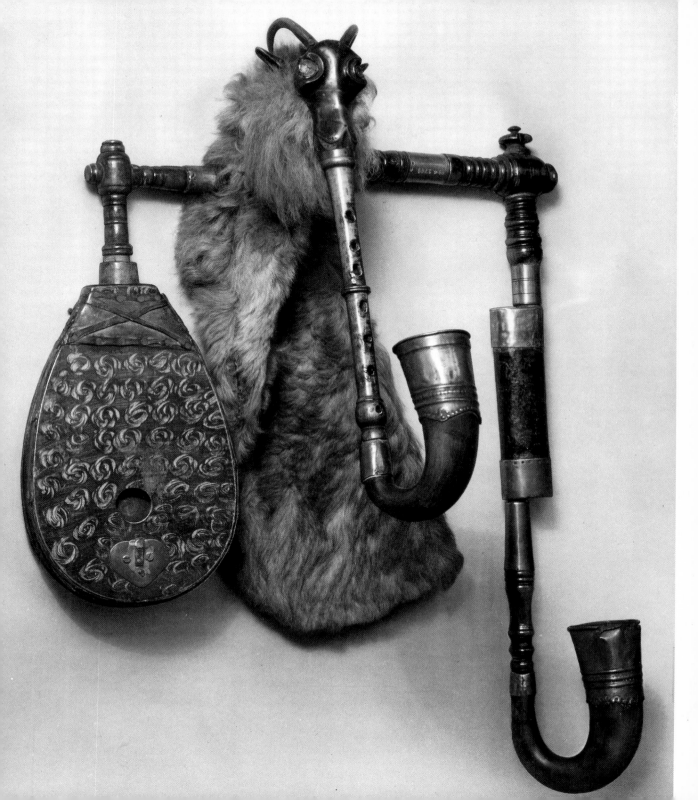

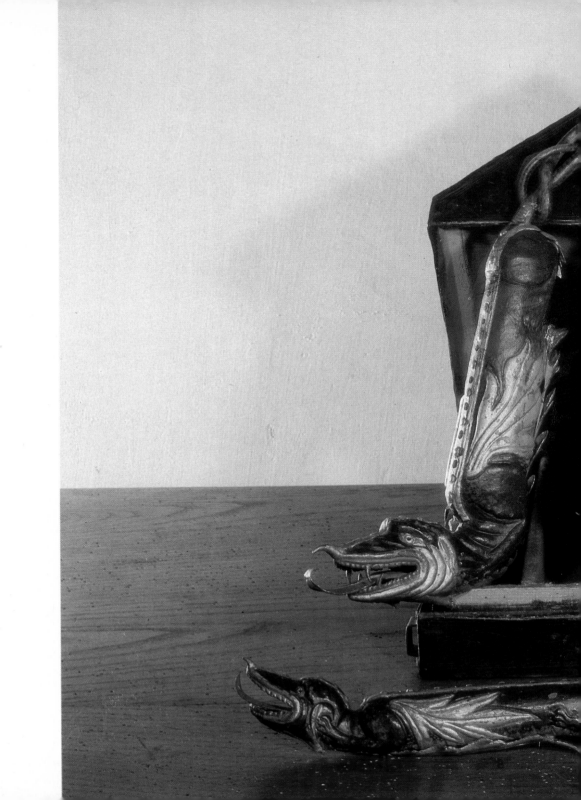

106 Upright piano (pianino), Pierre Érard, Paris, 1834; Paris, Musée de l'Opéra.

107 Double bass (detail), Giovanni Battista Dini, Lucignano, 1707; Leipzig, Musikinstrumenten-Museum der Karl-Marx-Universität.

108 Treble recorders (details), German, c. 1730; Leipzig, Musikinstrumenten-Museum der Karl-Marx-Universität.

Overleaf:
109 Lyre-harp, Italian, Carlo Scalfi, first half of the 19th century; New York, Metropolitan Museum of Art.

The oldest of these instruments was the *clavichord* (I2221) which developed from the monochord ("one string") of the ancient Greeks; in the Middle Ages extra strings were added (in 1323 John de Muris mentioned one with four strings which could produce 19 different tones). Towards the end of the 14th century keys replaced the human fingers as the plucking mechanism. Inspired by the organ which was now becoming popular, the clavichord appeared (Latin clavis = key), (Greek chordé = string). The early variant was termed "fretted"; each string served from two to five different keys by being struck at various places. At the far end of each key was a tangent (Latin- "touching") which struck the desired string from below and thereby divided it into one freely vibrating part which actually produced the sound and another section which was dampened via a coating of felt or other material. It was not until 1700 that the fret-free variant came onto the scene: each note and key now had its own string (and soon two). In spite of its limited volume, the clavichord remained popular well into the 18th century. By agitating the key, the string could be caused to oscillate and thus produce a trembling sound known as "vibrato", rather like the warbling effect of a human voice. This possibility of modulating the sound was partially equalled with the development of the hammer mechanism since the tone could not be altered. This was also the reason why composers such as Johann Sebastian Bach and his son Carl Philipp Emanuel held the clavichord to be the equal of the harpsichord; C. P. E. Bach even wrote his famous study of it (1753 and 1762). The multi-stringed monochord (to be precise, the polychord) developed into the clavichord through the addition of the organ keyboard. In a similar fashion the psaltery, which in contradistinction to the "polychord" has strings of various lengths, was also fitted with keys that plucked the strings by means of plectra (the quills of crows or thorns). Thus arose the second sub-group (I2222), the *harpsichord*. On this new instrument, the tone quality could not be varied, but this disadvantage was offset by a gain in volume, tonal richness and its ability to harmonise with the timbres of string and wind instruments.

Among the harpsichord family, we distinguish between spinets and wing-shaped harpsichords depending on the alignment of the strings with respect to the keys. The *spinet* (Italian from Latin spina = thorn) or *virginal* (from Latin virga = twig, rod, stick) had a rectangular box-like case with the keys at right angles to the strings. The keys increased in length in accordance with the distance away from the keyboard of the relevant string. Double coursing and the desire to extend the size of the sound-box soon led to the second variant by which strings and keys were parallel, with the result that all the keys were equally short: the strings decreased in length from left (the bass end) to right (the treble end), thus giving the *harpsichord* (French *clavecin*, German *Kielflügel*) its classic wing shape which survives to this day in the form of the concert grand. Among the most famous harpsichord makers was the Ruckers dynasty which was founded by Hans the Elder, who died in 1625.

Double instruments were also experimented with at an early stage. At first, separate small virginals (single virginals, spinettino, ottavina) were made with a four-foot compass (i. e. an octave higher than the normal eight-foot keyboard) and coupled with the main instrument (double virginal, spinet). Sometimes, the strings were double coursed, meaning each key was connected both to a four-foot and an eight-foot string. By means of a special stop taken over from the organ, the two courses could then be separated. Hans Ruckers the Elder made the first double manual harpsichords, which were usually equipped with several registers (at first hand stops and later pedals, too), including one which could transpose upwards by an octave (four-foot) and downwards (16-foot) and the lute stop, by means of which a strip of felt dampened the strings immediately as they were struck. Further refinements were added in the middle of the 18th century in the form of a stop made from the skin of an ox's tongue and a shutter (copied from the swell-work of the organ) allowing the timbre and volume to be further modified.

A relatively rare variant of the harpsichord was the *cembalo verticale* or *clavicytherium*; it has an upright soundbox (cp. the giraffe piano which was the vertical form of the pianoforte). The advantages were obvious: it took up less space, the sound waves—which were never all that strong—reached both player and listener directly, and lastly, it provided new and larger surfaces for decorative purposes. The main drawback was the high price. A tricky engineering problem was involved: whereas on normal horizontally strung harpsichords, the jacks fell back into place under the force of gravity after striking the strings from below with their quills, on clavicytheria a special mechanism had to be designed to do this job.

The clavichord (both fretted and fret-free) and the harpsichord (including the spinet and virginal) left their mark on an entire musical era and initiated a process of development in music which was given sterling support by the viol and violin before reaching a triumphant culmination with the advent of the pianoforte.

The *pianoforte* (I2223) forms the third sub-group. It combines the wing-shaped form of the harpsichord (the less common square piano was more akin to the spinet in shape) with a mechanism that imitated the dulcimer. The sole difference was that the hammers (unlike the dulcimer's jacks) struck the string from below, thereby regaining in part the tonal dexterity which had been lost by the harpsichord. Putting it simply, one may say that the pianoforte inherited the volume (which it soon greatly increased) and the outward form of the harpsichord. From the clavichord, it inherited the ability in part to modify the volume (though not the tone). Although the harpsichord and clavichord continued on the scene until 1800, three instrument makers in three different countries had already begun work on the revolutionary new invention a century earlier. Today Bartolomeo Cristofori from Florence is given the main credit for inventing the piano in preference to the Frenchman Marius and the Saxon Schroeter; three of the pianos he made between 1720 and 1722 still exist.

In Germany, other craftsmen soon turned their attention to the new invention, including Gottfried Silbermann from Freiberg (the instruments he made aroused the interest of J. S. Bach) and Christian Ernst Friederici of Gera.

The mechanism of the pianoforte underwent many changes in the long course of its development. Initially, there were two different systems: Christofori's double action and the Viennese action which survived until 1850. Both had a simple escapement, i. e. a mechanism

for returning the hammer immediately after impact to its starting position ready to strike again. When the English adopted the double action for their very modestly priced square pianos, they rejected the relatively expensive escapement mechanism, so that the Viennese action, represented by Silbermann of Strasbourg and J. A. Stein of Augsburg, took the lead. Stein built his first grand pianoforte with a Viennese action in 1773; his daughter married the pianist Streicher and founded a firm in Vienna which soon became famous. Meanwhile, the English action had now also been fitted with an escapement and under Broadwood even led the field for a time: when Beethoven demanded an instrument with greater volume from Streicher the latter referred him to Broadwood! But the most brilliant innovation of all came from Paris: in 1823 Sébastien Érard (b. Strasbourg in 1752) invented the repetition action or double escapement. Now the hammer did not fully return to its resting position. Until the key was released, it remained poised half way in order to repeat the stroke quickly as required. Liszt's brilliant piano pieces, in particular, would have been unthinkable without this innovation. Érard also strengthened the strings and hammer heads.

The increased strain was soon too much for the wooden frame to bear. After initial experimentations with frames reinforced with iron supports, the Americans produced a frame made completely of iron; the German immigrant Steinweg, whose name was anglicised to Steinway in 1864, then invented cross-stringing whereby the bass strings were stretched over the treble strings and made to produce maximum sympathetic vibrations on depressing a pedal. The world famous firms of Steinway, Blüthner and Bechstein were all founded around the middle of the century, to be followed later by Förster.

Two alternatives regarding the alignment of the strings introduced some variety into the almost monotonous technological progress of the pianoforte. Firstly, the *square piano*: its strings ran at right angles to the keys like those of the clavichord, spinet and virginal. The oldest square piano dates back to 1742. It was particularly popular in England. By 1835 its compass, helped by its shape and its ability to be placed flush to the wall, was six and a half octaves. Finally, the square piano also established itself in America. Its advantage with regard to the pianino (which eventually won the day and became the modern "piano") was self-evident: the player could see over the top and could also himself be seen by the audience.

The second variant, like the clavicytherium, had an upright frame with strings running parallel to the keys. It was pioneered by the aforementioned Friederici: he built his *pyramid piano*, the case of which formed a giant symmetrical triangle, in Gera in 1745. It had shutters which were opened during a performance, and curved sides. However, after 1825 the fashion was for straight sides, a square pyramidal shape—often topped by vases—and for the solid case with hinged panels to be replaced by a more open frame with metal struts. Closely related to it was the *lyre piano*, which incorporated a symbolic lyre-shape and also had a strictly symmetrical outline. For a time, there was another variant with the asymmetrical shape of a harp whose base strings were often surmounted by a scroll resting on an impressive classical pillar.

The last and most successful variant of the pianoforte in its vertical form was the *pianino*. To save space the frame rested on the floor instead of starting at keyboard level and the strings were overstrung. The development of this "grand piano substitute"—which is what we should actually call the popular upright piano—was mainly the work of American and English craftsmen, who even by 1800 were making use of a massive iron frame; the model devised by Wornum of London in 1826 is still largely the one we use today.

Curious and numerous set-backs resulted from attempts to produce the sound not by striking and dividing the string with a tangent (as on the clavichord), nor by plucking it with a jack (as on the harpsichord and spinet), nor yet by striking it with a hammer (as on the pianoforte), but by rubbing the strings with a looped bow (either by a rosined band or by a wheel coated with parchment). The idea for this *piano-violin* which forms the fourth sub-group (I2224) of the pianofortes, was born of the desire to simulate a chamber orchestra of strings through a single keyboard instrument plus player. Its supporters were both mistaken and disap-

pointed since one of the basic criteria for achieving the sound of a stringed instrument, namely the typical formation of the individual note and of the melodic line by the action of the bow with all the resultant consequences for the articulation, was impossible on a polyphonically played keyboard.

Belonging to the family of the compound chordophones (II) were those instruments whose soundboxes could not be separated from the strings without destroying the sound: the viols (including both viols and violins—II313), the lutes (including the guitars—II32) and the harps (II4). Apart from the stringed keyboard instruments which we have just examined, they are of the most interest to us. The first two groups—*tromba marina* (II1) and the *lyre* (II2) are only of historical importance. The lute family (II3) has the greatest variety of members. Here we must distinguish between those with inferior and those with frontal stringholders.

Those with inferior stringholders (II31) or those whose strings were affixed not to the belly but to the lower rib or base of the instrument comprised the hurdygurdies and rebecs (mini-violins), all plucked instruments descended from the fiddle (which itself belongs to the violin family), and—most importantly for the development of European instrumental music—the viols.

The *hurdy-gurdy* (II311) had a soundbox which was an historical compromise between a fiddle, flat box and lute; it had one or two melody strings running over the soundbox which were stopped (depressed) by keys as opposed to the finger. They were hidden from view by being enclosed in a box mounted on the belly. They were flanked by between one and four drone strings, and they all ran from the bottom end of the instrument (end-pin) over a rotating wheel, which acted as the looped bow, up to the frontal peg-box, that was normally surmounted by a carved head. Detailed descriptions of it from the 10th century survive: for example, it is depicted on a stained glass window in the cathedral of Chartres. The prototype was about four and a half feet long and normally required two people to play it. Originally, the hurdy-gurdy was a kind of mechanised fiddle; at first it was known as an "organistrum", the "lira"—an archaic term for the fiddle with a secondary meaning of "turn". For a while, it was given a simple square box shape instead of the fiddle outline, and after 1700, it emerged with its lute-shaped body and a very short neck.

The *kleine Geige* ("small violin") bore little resemblance to the modern violin, but was rather the European descendant of the *rebec* or *rubebe* (from the Arabic rabâb) which was still being played in 14th century Spain (II312). A later member of this family was the *kit* or *pochette*, which incorporated all the essential features of this type: inferior stringholder, lateral pegs, and a pear-shaped soundbox which merged with the neck. One early representation showed, albeit anachronistically, Apollo holding the aristocratic fiddle while Marsyas has a rebec—its reputation was almost obscene.

The all-important viol family (II313) with its subgroups of the fiddle, viol and violin goes back to the *fiddle (vielle*; II3131). It developed from Asiatic (Turkestan) and Balkan/Slavonic prototypes. In the Balkans, it was known as the "lira", probably owing to Byzantine influence and because it was one of several different instruments which derived from the classical lyre. This misleading term then found its way via the Mediterranean to Italy. By 1300, the original shallow carved soundbox had been replaced by a series of ribs which were then glued together, and the soundbox acquired the deep bowl shape of the lute and became waisted to give the bow easier access to the strings. As a rule, one or two of the five or six strings were drones which ran along the side of the instrument. (The term "drone" meant from 1270 onwards a freely vibrating and unstopped string, and later came to refer to the constantly vibrating deep string of unvarying pitch of the hurdy-gurdy and the deep pipe of the bagpipes.) The seven strings necessitated a heart or leaf-shaped frontal peg-box and an extreme indentation of the waist so that the bow could be drawn across all the strings together when required. This instrument, the full name of which was *lira da braccio* ("arm fiddle") was also capable of producing polyphonous effects. The *lira da gamba* ("leg fiddle") was a later bass variant with between nine and thirteen melody strings and two drones.

The second largest sub-group in the viol family after the fiddles were the *viola da gambas* or *viols* for short (II3132). They had slanting shoulders connecting the neck and waist, seven frets, higher ribs but a flat back, often C-holes and six strings. The way they were constructed gave them their strangely muted sound. In the Renaissance and early Baroque, there was a demand for a homogeneous consort of instruments of varying sizes just like a human choir. As a result, a five-stringed sub-bass viol was produced around 1580 which was over two metres tall. The normal-sized viola da gamba was held between the legs. Unlike the cello it had no spike for resting it on the floor. The back was sloped at the top so as not to hinder the player. The increase in the number and tension of the strings required a bent-back peg-box with lateral pegs—unlike the lira da braccio or fiddle but clearly in keeping with the principles on which the rebec was constructed.

The *viola bastarda* was a combination of viola da gamba and lira da gamba produced by the Italian Renaissance; its characteristic feature was the rose (sound-hole) of the lyre and of the plucked instruments. Another reminder of the lyre was the presence of sympathetic strings of thin wire which ran under the melody strings—this was a technical device copied from the Orient. Typical of this group was the *baryton*. With its six to seven strings and the shape of the soundbox, it was more of a bass viol (i. e. a bass viola da gamba). But like the viola d'amore, it also had ten or more sympathetic strings of metal, which not only vibrated freely like those of the viola d'amore but could also be plucked by the player's left thumb from behind the neck. A second neck ran parallel to the first, and the sympathetic strings ran unseen behind it to the peg-box; this also made the instrument more stable since the total of at least sixteen strings put a considerable strain on the neck. As far as the etymology of the name is concerned, it is now believed that the original designation of "viola bardone" had nothing to do with the modern baritone voice but rather derived from the "bordone" (see Leopold Mozart, for example), which was a reference to the freely vibrating (or "bordun") string.

Its treble counterpart was the *viola d'amore*, an alto viola bastarda with between five and seven melody strings (of gut) and between seven and fourteen sympathetic strings (of wire) which, as on the baryton, ran underneath the melody strings and finger-board. It was characterised by flame-shaped sound-holes and usually terminated in a carved head which often depicted Cupid with his eyes blindfolded.

The third sub-group, which has produced the modern violin, viol, cello and—as a "half-breed" (according to Curt Sachs)—the double bass, is the *viola da braccio* (II3133), which seems to have developed from the lira da braccio, the most highly developed member of the fiddle family. By 1590, it had more or less attained its present form. Whereas the viola da gamba developed from a bass instrument, the forerunner of the violin family was an alto instrument—the *viola*. The plain and practical perfection of the *violin* was achieved via a long period of development during the lifetime of the maestros of Cremona and Brescia: Maggini, Amati, Stradivari and the Guarneri dynasty. Subsequently, there were no great or remotely comparable further improvements to the violin. However, there were some interesting offshoots, such as the French *quinton* (from the Latin for "fifth voice"), a five-stringed instrument developed in the 18th century, and various attempts to raise the pitch of the viola by also adding a fifth string: the *violino pomposo* and other creations of the 18th century.

The modern *cello* met stiff competition in the tenor viol, which was preferred as a virtuoso instrument. Of all the members of the viol family, it survived the longest—until 1800. In its early stage of development, the cello normally had to render service as a continuo instrument, where it had to provide the obligatory bass accompaniment while the tenor viol played the solo parts. J. S. Bach's *viola pomposa* (violoncello piccolo) was a smaller version with five strings and a tonal range extended upwards. In its German form, the *double bass* only half belongs to the violin family. Its short neck, tapered upper bout and body flattened at the top are strangely reminiscent of the viola da gamba. The Italian bass, on the other hand, followed the violin pattern. The last sub-group of this family of instruments with inferior stringholders (the first of which were the hurdy-gurdies, the second the *kleine Geige*, and the third the viola plus fiddle, viol and violin) comprises those derivatives of the fiddle which, unlike the first sub-group of the viols, were not bowed but plucked (II314). Included

under this heading are the sub-groups cittern, guitar, mandolin, mandora and mandola.

The *cittern* combined a flat pear-shaped (occasionally bell-shaped) arched body carved like a lute (though unlike the lute it had an inferior stringholder); initially it had frontal pegs but from the 17th century onwards lateral ones, and usually possessed a double course of strings (up to 12 wire strings). The *arch-cittern* was a variant produced after 1600, which also had a large number of drone strings that were affixed to a second "collar" on the neck. The *mandolin* has existed in its modern form from around 1650. It can be distinguished from the guitar by the fact that its strings are affixed to the end-pin, by its arched body, steel strings and by the fact that it is played with a plectrum. Particularly in view of the last point, it is believed that it originated from Persia.

In considering the compound chordophones (II) we have so far concentrated almost exclusively on the lute family (II3) and then only on the latter's sub-group—instruments with inferior stringholders (II31). The group of instruments with frontal stringholders (II32) spawned far fewer offspring; apart from the Renaissance instruments *colascione* and *pandora* it comprised the two groups of the lutes and guitars.

Starting in the 14th century and culminating in the 15th century, the lute (II321) was at the centre of European musical life and was thus the equivalent, so to speak, of the piano in the domestic households of the time; abundant use was also made of its polyphonic potential. Like the name, the prototype originated in the Arab world (al'ûd = wood), even though it was given its classic form in Europe (possibly by the Spanish Moors). Its main features were its arched body without sides and with a back usually made of nine (up to a maximum of 33) ribs glued together, its bent-back neck with lateral pegs, its single sound-hole, its fretted finger-board, and its frontal stringholder on the belly. In the course of the 16th century, it developed its classic form with eleven (gut) strings and eight frets. At the same time, greater stress was laid upon rich decoration and on increasing its volume. Selective use was made of materials such as maple, yew, pine wood, ebony, brazil wood, cypress wood and sandalwood, Indian cane, whalebone and ivory. The number of strings increased from twelve to twice that amount! Like the viol family, a whole group of lutes developed in which even the bass was represented.

Its demise came about in the 17th century, first in Italy where in the form of the *archlute*, it had tried to impress by its exuberant drone effects, and in France. It survived longest in Germany before finally succumbing to the keyboard instruments around the time of Bach's death.

The drone strings, which were the essential feature of the *archlute*, needed a second peg-box or collar, just like the arch-cittern. Three variants of the archlute emerged and were distinguished by the position of this second peg-box: the *theorbe* (etymology uncertain) on which the main peg-box was not bent back and the secondary peg-box was placed slightly to one side; the *theorboe-lute* (normally a lute which was later modified), which had a bent-back main peg-box and a curved secondary collar; and the *chittarone*, which was a giant theorboe with an extremely long neck connecting the two peg-boxes, thereby increasing the height of the instrument to as much as two metres.

In its early form, the *guitar* (II322) was a mixture of European and Moorish traditions with occasionally lateral pegs, but by the 17th century, it had attained its definitive form: rear pegs and five strings (a sixth was added in the 18th century). It was so easy to tune and play the guitar, especially after the initial double coursing was abandoned, that by the beginning of the 19th century, it had become a truly folk instrument. Its name represents a cultural link with the past going back over many centuries: Greek kithára, Arabic qîtâra, Spanish guitarra. The *lyre-guitar* was a normal six-stringed guitar fashioned to look like the classical kithara; this made it more difficult to play, but was attractive to look at. *Lute-guitars* combined the body of a lute (with several roses) with the frets, strings and peg-box of the guitar.

The oldest group within the compound chordophones is the *harp* family (II4); they are depicted on Sumerian reliefs of 3500 B. C. Their essential features have not altered but merely been improved.

The *arched harp* was followed by the *angular harp*; in Europe the *frame harp* was then invented by the 8th century with the addition of a frontal pillar to these early prototypes. The European forms have a triangular shape with narrow apex and are made up of three sections: the front pillar, the neck with tuning pins (their alignment is the same as on the modern grand piano), and the soundbox which slopes down to the base of the pillar. The harps are subdivided into two groups in accordance with the pitch: *chromatic* (one string per semitone) and *distonic* harps (tuned to the major mode)—(II431–II432). The latter group includes the two variants, the *hooked harp* (by tuning a hook each string could be shortened and so raised in pitch by a semi-tone) and the *pedal-harp*. The pedal-harp had a set of pedals which worked a mechanism (which was sometimes visible behind a glass front) by means of which all notes of the same pitch (e. g. all the C notes) could be raised by a semi-tone, though no flat keys could then be played. For this reason, the inventive harpsichord and pianoforte maker Érard devised the double pedal-harp in 1810; depending on whether the pedals were fully or only half depressed all the strings could be raised by either one or two semi-tones. This is why the basic key of the strings is C flat major. At the beginning of the 19th century, fierce rivalry broke out between the hooked harp and the (double) pedal-harp. The most vigorous champion of the former was its inventor Henri Naderman (son of a Parisian publisher and harp maker and brother of a royal virtuoso on, and composer for, the harp). In the end, however, its bulkiness proved too awkward to be carried around by hand and Érard's more compact model won the day—in one year the Strasbourg-based maker reached a turnover of 25,000 pounds sterling through the sale of his harps alone.

Appendix

Selected Bibliography

Besseler, Heinrich: *Musik des Mittelalters und der Renaissance.* Potsdam (1931).

Bragard, R., and J. de Hen: *Musikinstrumente aus zwei Jahrtausenden.* Stuttgart, 1968.

Buchner, Alexander: *Musikinstrumente der Völker.* Prague, 1968.

Buchner, Alexander: *Musikinstrumente im Wandel der Zeiten.* Prague, 1956.

Buchner, Alexander: *Musikinstrumente von den Anfängen bis zur Gegenwart.* Prague, 1971.

Flor, Peters: *Die niederländische Orgelkunst.* Antwerp, 1971.

Hamann, Richard: *Geschichte der Kunst.* Berlin, 1963 and 1965.

Handbuch der Musikwissenschaft. Ed. Ernst Bücken, Potsdam (1929), particularly the articles "Instrumentenkunde" by Wilhelm Heinitz and "Musik der Antike" by Curt Sachs.

Henkel, Hubert: *Kielinstrumente.* Leipzig, 1979.

Hirt, Franz Josef: *Meisterwerke des Klavierbaus.* Olten, 1955.

Jahn, Johannes: *Wörterbuch der Kunst.* Stuttgart, 1940.

Minkwitz, Johannes: *Illustriertes Taschenwörterbuch der Mythologie aller Völker.* Leipzig, 1856.

Moritz, Karl Philipp: *Götterlehre.* Leipzig, 1972.

Moser, H. J.: *Musiklexikon in zwei Bänden.* Hamburg, 1955—1963.

Musik in Geschichte und Gegenwart. Edited by F. Blume. Kassel and Basel, 1949—1973.

Otterbach, Friedemann: *Schöne Musikinstrumente.* Munich, 1975.

Rheims, Maurice: *Kunst um 1900.* Vienna-Munich, 1971.

Riemann: *Musiklexikon.* Mainz, 1959—1975.

Sachs, Badstübner, Neumann: *Christliche Ikonographie in Stichworten.* Leipzig, 1973.

Sachs, Curt: *Handbuch der Musikinstrumentenkunde.* Leipzig, 1930.

Schäfer, Ernst: *Laudatio Organi. Eine Orgelfahrt von der Ostsee bis zum Erzgebirge.* Leipzig, 1972.

Schrammeck, Winfried: *Museum Musicum.* Leipzig, 1976.

Valentin, Erich: *Handbuch der Instrumentenkunde.* Regensburg, 1963.

Weltgeschichte in Daten. Berlin, 1973.

Winternitz, Emanuel: *Die schönsten Musikinstrumente des Abendlandes.* Munich, 1966.

Zoozmann, Richard: *Zitate- und Sentenzenschatz der Weltliteratur alter und neuer Zeit.* Leipzig (after 1911).

Index of Names

Unitalicised numbers refer to text pages, numbers in italics to illustrations.

Sources of Illustrations